David Walter Purdie

Poems and songs

David Walter Purdie

Poems and songs

ISBN/EAN: 9783744723114

Printed in Europe, USA, Canada, Australia, Japan

Cover: Foto ©Thomas Meinert / pixelio.de

More available books at **www.hansebooks.com**

POEMS AND SONGS

BY

DAVID W. PURDIE

"THE ETTRICK BARD."

SELKIRK:
GEORGE LEWIS & CO.
MDCCCXCVII.

TO THE RIGHT HONOURABLE

THE EARL OF DALKEITH

THIS VOLUME IS DEDICATED

BY HIS

FAITHFUL AND DUTIFUL SERVANT

THE AUTHOR.

PREFACE.

COURTEOUS READER,

The favourable reception which my little book, published twelve years ago, met with has induced me to appear again before you soliciting your patronage. I have no time-worn excuses to offer in presenting my literary venture; I have published on my own responsibility, and am prepared to take your verdict—be it good or bad.

In reviewing my poems, I only ask the critic to bear in mind that the author is not a cultured scholar, but an unlettered son of toil. I thank most cordially my subscribers, one and all, for their munificent patronage towards my humble flights in song; as without such generous aid this volume could not have been before you.

Go forth my book to die or live,
    Though fame should never crown thee,
My first love and my last, believe
    I 'm not ashamed to own thee.

DAVID W. PURDIE.

BROCKHILL, ETTRICK,
    April, 1897.

CONTENTS.

———

POEMS AND SONGS.

Spring.

'T is spring-time of the year.   A jolly time,
When every thing in Nature scents new birth,
And takes on life anew.   The infant bud,
Nursed in its leafy cradle, lays aside
Its weaning robes, flirts with the fickle sun,
And weds at last a ripe maturity.
From lofty boughs the voice of Spring is heard
Rejoicing in the glory of the year ;
Wild flowers dismiss the bandages of death,
And, flattered by the blandishments of youth,
Are coaxed to life again.
                              The green kirtle
Of Nature is spread over all the hills,
Until their ample sides are clothed with sheep
Nibbling the juicy blade, startling the hare,
Who scuds arrowy up the rising ground,
Her speed her sole protection ; she is soon
Lost to view, where in the quiet uplands
She may rove and browse at sweetest pleasure.

A

The coil'd adder, ugly and repulsive,
Wriggles a passage through the length'ning grass,
The terror of the shepherd.   Even collie,
Ready on all occasions to defend
His canine rights against an open foe,
He hears the dreaded hiss, and looks alarmed,
With ruffled back he edges from the sound ;
By instinct taught it is no level match,
He wisely leaves the reptile all alone.
The lively squirrel, scamp'ring o'er the sward,
When danger threatens knows a safe retreat
On yon tall larch.   Nimbly, by corkscrew route,
He scales the steep incline, pausing anon
To scan the movements of the enemy
Below ; yet unrelaxed his vigilance—
The faintest motion hurries on his flight
To heights serene, where he in safety sits
Secure from all his foes.
                              The shy cuckoo,
The trumpeter of Spring, again returns
To cheer the rustic swain, who, list'ning oft
To catch the name resounding o'er the dale,
Hastes when he hears it, hoping he is first
The welcome news to tell.   The busy bee,
Run short of stores, with idleness enforced
In winter's cheerless days, in sunny hours
With ceaseless toil forages for her wants,
So lavishly provided, storing up
With miser care the yellow hoards so rich,
Teaching improvident man a lesson

In the useful art of thrift.   The ploughboy,
Turning o'er the soil, whose broad bosom soon
Shall fertilise the seed, beguiles the dull
Monotony of toil with lays of love,
That speak the virtues of some winsome maid
That he is sweet upon, longs for the tryst,
The twilight hour, when they shall meet again ;
When truthful lips, untaught to coin a lie,
Shall yet once more rehearse the play of love,
That ne'er grows old with age.   Happy Eden !
Where the most sacred of all knots was tied,
The first of untold numbers, and untroubled
With the delicacy of selection,
Adam's courtship would be a happy one.

In scarlet coat, with white top boots and spurs
Gracing a shapely leg, the huntsman bold,
Well mounted, gallops o'er the level plain
With his unruly pack, bent on the death
Of a May fox, the trophy of the chase.
The schoolmaster, forgetting not that once
He was a boy himself, lets out the school
To see the hunt, the king of British sports ;
Himself a sporting man, swift in his mind
He weighs the action, substance, bone, and build
Of every noble steed ; then totals up
The major points, and with unerring skill
He spots his horse, on whose speed he would bet
A tidy sum, had he the same to ride.
The gay hedgerows, in holiday attire,

Become the rendezvous of joyous birds,
Rearing the cherished young. In sheltered forks,
Hid from the prying eye of truant boy,
Intent on pillage; for the speckled prize
May please a comrade stronger than himself
Of whom he stands in awe. The tea-cup cot
With patient skill is dexterously built—
Could human hands do better? Maternal
Care, unwearied, hatches out the brood, while
The male bird caters for the household wants.
Confusion seize the hand who senselessly
Would rob a wild bird's nest; the poor, mean thief
Deserves not pity, but the lash of law
Rigorously applied.
                    The fresh milkmaid,
Whose willing hands invite the milk to flow
From Cherry's udder, singing as she milks—
A pretty picture, fair as spring itself—
Her dark eyes so enchanting. Shepherd John
Is shadowed by them; yet he often sees
In pale moonlight the wish of all his dreams
So eloquently told that well might make
The babbling poet dumb. Star of the soul,
What tongue can rival thee for speaking truth,
Or letting secrets out that should be kept?
Athwart the daisied fields the bonny lambs,
Untrammell'd by the weighty cares of age,
Forsake the ready teat, and headlong plunge
Into the sports of youth. Not long enjoyed,
For soon the fatal knife shall spoil the life;

Hung in a well-kept shop, in dainty cuts
Meant for the rich—the poor man knows thee not.
Thy high-condition'd carcase is doled out
To fatten him who has the lengthen'd purse,
But needs thy aid the least.   -
                          The chill east wind,
The fierce companion of our northern spring,
Hunts out rheumatic bones with savage zest,
And plagues the tender chest, feeding the grave,
Which, greedy, folds within its silent walls
The strangest crowd of all.   The sexton, grave
As his occupation, makes no complaint.
When busy seasons press, pockets his fee
With nonchalance sublime—it is his trade,
And harder than the marble is the heart
By usage steel'd against the claims of grief.
The snowdrop white, the virginal of spring,
Unsullied as the snow-wreath newly made
At yon dyke side, when urging winds compel
The spotless flakes to form one glittering mass,
Emerges from the tomb of enforced death,
And gladly comes to tell a bleak, bare world
Of beauty hid, that time alone reveals.
Impulsive man, restrain thy headstrong haste;
Thou canst do nothing were 't not done for thee:
In patience wait; learn from the little flower
That God is good, and doeth all things well.
The singing stream that winds through meadows
        green,
High-coloured with the soft, refreshing rain,

The urchin tempts to try his angling skill:
With willow wand, a piece of ragged twine,
And pin half bent, whereon a laggard worm
Is dangling hung, he plies the peaceful art
With rich success, and carries home at eve,
With prideful look, a string of glossy fish
That ancient veterans in the noble craft,
Too little practised, oft sigh for in vain.
O, sweetest scene! amidst the purest calm,
The gorgeous wealth of Nature is displayed.
Here no distressing sameness greets the eye,
But lovely shades no canvas ever knew,
So exquisitely bloom; the brilliant dew
That balls each blade of grass, shines with a blaze
That shames the diamond mine, where brawny arms
Unwearied toil to find the precious gem.
Sweet primrose bank, where roving children climb
When unappreciated tasks are done,
And schoolbags banished till another day.
With eager haste the tiny hands explore
The yellow blooms, selecting them with care;
Tied in a bunch, in cooling water, clear,
On window-sill, refreshing all the room;
They appetise the meal, when from his work
The toiler comes to rest at evening's close.
The gardener hails with joy the swift return
Of omens bright that hint work is at hand.
The swelling gale sports with the swirling clouds
Of powder'd dust, and dries the earth again.
With labour'd toil he delves the whitening soil,

And spreads the hillock beds in truthful squares,
Smooth as a sea becalmed.   Dimpled with smiles,
The gathering sun peeps o'er the stalwart wall,
Whose back is lined with cultivated trees—
Cherry and apple, plum and jargonelle,
The emperor of pears, spread like a fan,
To grasp the heat that forces on the fruit,
Whose luscious taste doth tempt the plundering hand
To depredation make.   Pest of his life,
The weed, undaunted, heedless of rebuffs,
Persists to mar the loveliest of plots,
Where richest flowers in sweet confusion grow,
And gorgeous terraces, delight of all!

O lovely Spring! when slumbering earth awakes
From her long sleep, and marshals all her strength
To set her beauty forth.   Imposing pageant!
What vast resources are at thy command,
Of every shape and hue, and size and form;
All know their place; and, when the call goes forth,
With swift intelligence each plant, each flower,
Becomes a holy thing.   Admirable!
In contemplation lost, we look with awe
Through thee up to the Maker of them all;
Great Power divine, whose sovereign will is law,
Beyond dispute, through boundless realms of space.
Bounteous Nature, the first of teachers,
Thy information unimpeachable,
Thy smallest atom has a kernel sweet,
Primed with instruction!   Let attentive eyes

And willing ears, open for improvement,
Take note of thee ; though dumb, thou hast a tongue
That cannot err.   O dim, unsettled mind,
Erratic upon the main point of life ;
Wearied soul, that fain would find a haven,
An anchorage safe, why dost thou wander
'Mid clouded doubts, with clearest truth so near,
And free to all.   Priceless of gifts ! with thee
The ocean of life, smooth as a mill pond,
No raging winds explore; all is so calm.
And, when the end comes, the exit is peace ;
And in a purer sphere the soul shall know
Undreamt-of joys.   A Spring-time ever there.

Friendship.

Friendship!   How sweet the name !   It smells of
    home,
With all the holy sweetness of the hearth,
The true abode of man.   What other name
Covers a heart so sympathetic, warm ?
The cream of the nobility of men
Are those who in affliction's darkest hour
Are not ashamed to help a brother man,
And drag him from the mire.   I have known such,
Although the crop is scarce, who willingly,

With hands as light as day, bestowed the gift
That made them friends indeed. How kind the heart
To whom want's tale is never told in vain!
With gratitude sincere I 'll ne'er forget
One honoured friend, who knew the poet's need,
And with unbounded liberality,
Unasked, which made it all the sweeter, gave,
With that frankness, wherein lies friendship's charm,
That looks for no return. If Coila's bard
Occasion had to eulogise Glencairn,
With double need have I to record here
My warmest thanks for such unlooked-for help
From one who, nameless, I hold not less dear.
I pity him who here had ample scope
To help his neighbour and who did it not—
Afraid to lose what never was his own,
But held in trust. When at the bar of Heaven;
The wretch quakes as he hears the charges read
In no faltering voice, justice is here,
And he gets it; but mercy's day is past.
So much is lost for what was worth so little.
The cowardly miser, whose fingers ache
Wrestling the coin, wasting the midnight oil
On devilish sport, forgets there is a God
That sees his sin, that some day shall avenge
His lack of love. O friendship, kindly thing,
Thy blessings are beyond the gift of kings.

Abram Lincoln.

Shades of Dante, Milton, Homer, Tasso,
Glorious mighty monarchs of the muse,
I have a theme, a hero nobler far
Than any chanted in those sweetest odes
Men call immortal.   A hero! yes,
A prince of heroes; yea, a king of men,
Abram Lincoln, the martyr President.
Called from the humblest rank in life to fill
A post that pedigreed kings might envy.
Ambition knew him not; laid out for him ·
Was higher, holier work than court intrigue;
His lifelong battle was with slavery,
Most Christian of wars.
                Shot like a felon
When his work was finished; but Death can not
Destroy the glory that surrounds his name.
Wherever manhood lives and virtue dwells,
Wherever Liberty erects her shrine,
There will heroic Lincoln be enthroned
Patron saint of freedom.   A man of men.
Hadst thou no other name, America,
Than his, it is enough to make thee great,
Although all else is lost in littleness.

General Sir Henry Havelock.

Brave Havelock's now no more.   We mourn a son,
As brave a man as ever mother bore.
Ready to die whene'er the summons came,
Death could not take him unawares.   He lived,
But feared it not; and when at last it came,
Mark well his words addressed to his dear son—
"Behold, see how a Christian man can die."
A soldier, too, he was.   Oft had he faced
The terror king in grimmest garb arrayed
On bloody battlefields, where human life
Was held as naught, that glory might be won.
On India's burning plain his troops he marched
Victorious amid the rebel hosts,
That no allegiance owned.   Onward, forward
He fought his way, and triumphed in the end;
But thousands slept in death, the price of war.
Now honours great were showered upon his head—
Who would dispute that they were not deserved?
No patent ever signed by royal hand
More worthier bestowed.   No victor's wreath
A nobler brow than Havelock's did adorn.
But Death's cold hand was near; he had escaped
War's perils to be smitten by a foe
Unseen, and more malignant.   Worn with disease,
His spirit fled in glory's brightest hour
From earth's frail tenement to wear the crown
And snow-white robe that wait the just on high.

Brown Eyes.

Brown eyes, sweet eyes, for seven long weary years
Thy glances bright annoyed my peace of mind.
No storm-toss'd bark upon the restless tide,
With land yet undiscovered, is more abroad
Than he who is in love.   Alternate swayed
By hopes and fears, uneasily he lives ;
And die he would unless bright-tinted hope
Rainbow'd the cloud and promised the reward.

The heart beats only in response to thine—
Love, priceless love, with all its joys, are mine.
Beautiful as the grass loaded with dew,
Bonny as the yellow primrose in spring,
Glorious as the silver moon set in blue,
Lovely and pure beyond the power to sing,
Is maiden's love in holy virgin bloom,
The light and life of the domestic home.

Brown Eyes, for thee my reverence is great ;
I owe thee a debt I can never pay ;
Thine was the incentive that made me sing ;
Love drew me out of self, and gave a breadth,
A purifying influence to life
That hath borne and shall bear fruit unto death.

Sweet Eyes, had I never met thee (and who
Dare say it was by merest chance I did ?
· Is there not a Providence in all things
That ordereth and ruleth well ?   There is.)

Poetic happiness had ne'er been mine.
Those who have never loved have never lived.
Thy tutelage shall live.   The strokes of Time,
That havoc plays with monuments of skill,
And wrecks at will the handiworks of man,
Shall fall with no distressing thud on thee.
Well sheltered in the mind the honey'd look,
Sweeter for remembrance, hath abiding
Lodgings.   Though I lost thee, yet I love thee—
Absent from sight, to sweet remembrance dear.

The Rich Man.

Clothed in the indolent ease of riches,
The man of wealth lounges his life away,
And murders precious time.   The fleeting hours,
That the swiftest racer could never catch,
Affording opportunities so grand
For doing good, are carelessly squander'd;
So lightly prized, out from our reach they slip,
Like sneaking thieves hurrying off the prize,
And like a shadow darting on the wall,
Not to be caught, are lost for evermore.
Seize every chance as it presents itself,
A sinew'd grasp keep on the latch of time,
Encourage every impulse hinting good,
Use the gold; 't was meant for circulation;
Not to feed the vanity of one man,

Nor lie useless under strong locks and keys,
To be examined as a doctor would
A sinking patient beyond human skill.
Rich man, you have a lot to answer for ;
Well may your soul be troubled at the brink
That leads to the beyond.   Afraid to pass
The surging deep where, on the other side,
Life's ledger shall be closely scrutinised.
Now is the time ; let not the sovereign hours
Slip idly by when so much could be done.
O, why delay ? the passport should be signed
When health is good, and not when sickness comes.
Scatter the dross 'mong the deserving poor,
'T was surely given that blessings might be done.
Then welcome waits you at the pearly gate
That opes to happiness—" Faithful servant,
Enter thou into the joy of thy Lord."

In Memoriam—The Earl of Dalkeith.

Upon a lone hill side, far from the haunts
Of busy men, the noble Earl died.
Sprung from a race renowned for martial deeds
And gallantry—the ancient clan of Scott—
Within his veins the best of blood did run,
Born to a high estate.   Noble by birth,
But nobler far the patent of the mind,

That only favoured few can ever wear.
Such coronet was his.   Beloved by all.
To rich and poor alike a brother man,
A comrade in their sorrows and their joys,
We mourn his death, more sad because of youth.
Ere yet the bud had blossom'd into fruit
The young chief lay cold in the shroud of death.

The Death of Mary.

My dear wife wasna lang spared to enjoy
The sweetness o' mairrit life; but we were
Happy the short while we were thegither.
If I was richt, a' was richt wi' Mary,
While endless were the schemes she invented
To make me what every man in his ain
Hoose should be—the happiest o' mortals.
But while we were baskin' in a' the sweet
Endearments o' hame, the Angel of Death
Was near; and Mary, my darling wife, was
Summoned into the presence of the King,
To abide wi' Him for ever.   A few
Meenits afore she dee'd, she ca'd me to
Her bedside, an' wi' a wistfu' look, fou
O' infinite tenderness, bade me watch
Ower the fragile bud that had that mornin'

Opened its wee een on a sinfu' world.
"Bob," she said (that was her favourite name
For me in the coortin' days), "promise me
That if the lassie an' you are spared, you
Will be kind till 'er for my sake, an' bring
Her up in the fear o' the Lord.   The world
And a' its frivolities are o' sma'
Accoont when it comes to a deein' hour.
Gin the maid fa's in love, as lasses will,
An' likes the lad as I aye likit you,
Let them mairry, Bob; it will ease my mind,
And make my deein' bed unco easy."
Taking my hand atween her ain lily
Anes, as white as snaw, an' gie'in' me her
Fareweel kiss, whispered softly in my ear—
"Bob, I 'll meet the lassie an' you in Heaven."
Thae were the last words she spoke, an', closin'
Her eyes as sweetly as a child gangs to
Sleep, a' that was mortal was left in my
Airms, while the immortal spirit o' my
Dearest and never-to-be-forgotten
Wife, peacefully wing'd its way to the high
And holy abodes o' bliss; where neither
Eye nor ear hath seen or heard the nameless
And sinless joys o' the heavenly hame.

The Losin' o' Grannie's Specs.

The other day auld Grannie dear
Had lost her specs, she kenned na where;
The like before had never been,
Sae carefu' was she ower her een.

Auld drawers were emptied inside oot,
And cupboard presses, withoot doot,
Had never been in sic a plicht
Since Grannie's happy bridal nicht.

Frae but tae ben she anxious gaed,
And mony a gey queer word she said,
Her speech was never meant for print—
To tell the truith, nae guid was in 't.

She ranged, and better ranged, the drawers,
And damaged sair the auld, dune spars;
But wad she drop?—ah, no; not she;
But ranged the mair persistently.

Another pair she 'd never get
That wad sae weel her vision fit,
The very best o' pebble gless,
They didna cost a penny less

Than ten and six. " Blind as a bat,
Me threed anither needle?   What?
Wee Davie's fots, the bonny lamb,
I 'll never see to feenish them."

B

An unco job.   Us bairns were wae;
We grat—what else can bairnies dae
When trouble comes?   'T was sic a fricht,
The thocht o' Grannie wantin' sicht!

Dispute this truith a' ye wha daur,
Things ne'er are got but where they are;
A peal of laughter loud arose—
The specs were found on Grannie's nose!

Unchanging Love.

True love, unchanging as yon mountain high,
   The sweetest joy the heart hath ever known;
Perhaps betrayed by one small, tiny sigh,
   More precious far because 't is all thine own.
Love is not love with a divided throne;
   It must be all in all before one shrine;
In sweet simplicity it stands alone,
   Like choicest vintage of the juicy vine;
   Nothing improves so much with age as love and
      wine.

Yon maid, whose teens are scarcely yet expired,
   Unripened beauty budding into form,
Behold that eye with true affection fired,
   The tender glance—how sweet, how kind, how
      warm!

Perchance an anxious mother takes alarm,
   The richness of her cheek bespeaks no good ;
Precautionary measures do no harm ;
    "Take plenty exercise and wholesome food—
   If these do not give health I do not know what
      should."

But, ah! fond mother, yet how very blind ;
   What! wilt thou be beneath deception's art ?
Hast thou forgot, or art thou not inclined
   To listen to the promptings of the heart ?
But at thy peril shun what would impart
   The greatest happiness the life could know.
Too late—sweet love hath flesh'd his fatal dart ;
   The die is cast, for either joy or woe.
   I would not sport with mine for all on earth below.

My Mother's Grave.

What memories crowd around me, as
   I stand where cowslips wave ;
O hallowed spot ! most dear of all ;
   It is my mother's grave.

With mingled feelings, I unbend
    Upon the grassy sod,
And meditate, with silent voice,
    Beside death's lone abode.

Methinks I see the loving look
    That watched my infant way,
Again I hear the sweetest voice
    That taught me how to pray.

She early on my mind impressed
    Wherein true greatness lay,
To sit loose by the things of earth,
    To walk the narrow way.

Can I forget the parting scene,
    The handshake, the good-bye,
The tryst to meet, when death no more
    Divides the family tie.

Sweet mother, dear, can fancy paint
    That hour of raptured joy,
You meet me at the Pearly Gate,
    To welcome home your boy.

In Memoriam.

In Loving and Affectionate Memory of my Dear Parents, William and Mary Purdie, who departed this Life on the 18th and the 24th of June, 1891, respectively, Aged 82 and 74 Years.

They are gone from this weary vale of woe,
To a brighter land in the world above,
Where the lives that were lovely here below
Are made sinless now by the hand of love.

They are gone from their children here on earth;
They were with us long, but the tie must cease;
May we, as we sit by the lonely hearth,
Pray that we, like them, may depart in peace!

'T was a happy change, though our grief was great;
The crown, the sweet harp, and the robe of white;
Neither eye nor ear can conceive the state,
Or the blissful joys in that land of light.

They are gone; may we follow in their train;
May we live, renewed by a holy faith,
So that none be lost, but all meet again,
In that happy home that shall know not death.

Brockhill.

Sweet sheltered spot!   From north, from east, from
    west
Wild storms may come, but cannot thee molest;
The kindly wood disarms each threatening foe,
And stubborn winds, all diadem'd in snow,
Deal gently with thee.   Here fairest flowers
In safety bloom in sweetly shaded bowers;
No frost, unkind, with icy fingers cold,
Dare throttle at the pride of Flora's fold.
Here genial spring, with mildest balmy dews,
Delights to shed the glory of her hues,
Where warbling birds, with closely feathered throats,
Enchant the hours with mellowest of notes.
The primrose stars add beauty to the green,
Where loveliness is to perfection seen.

Sweet residence—for twenty years my home—
Beneath thy roof I wrote my infant poem,
And straightway sent it to the local print;
The editor, with heart as hard as flint—
Although, no doubt, the deed was kindly meant—
Tormented it with fire.   I thanked him not,
'T was charity no author ever sought,
But ready found.   Yet happily I ween,
The dreamy hours beneath its spell have been
Long cut off from the world.   Now Kittlestrips,
The eely road that needed cautious steps,
Is pension'd off, a bridge usurps its place.

A thing of wire, equilibrium'd with grace,
O'erlooks the Ford, where salmon used to spawn,
Ere ottered steel conveyed them to the pan,
Where they became the wholesome food of man.

Communication open to the town,
With Ettrickbridge a suburb of thine own,
What may'st thou yet become! Alas, alas,
Sobriety forbids the random guess.
O hallow'd spot! where hottest youth outran
The boyhood race and slipp'd into the man;
Where staider joys did calmer warfare wage,
And gave the love subdued with sober age
The happy home, where soft endearments bright
Hedge in the life with Heaven's holy light.

Medley.

I climbed the " Braes o' Tullymet,"
    And there I gathered slaes,
And got acquaint wi' " Delvinside,"
    The king o' a' strathspeys.

" Sarah Drummond," too, was there,
    As also was " Miss Lyle,"
And then we entered " Kelvin Grove "
    In happy, first-rate style.

'Twas there I met the " Second Wife"
   O' my auld freend " Neil Gow,"
Next cam' the canty " Miller o' Drone"
   Wi' his white curly pow.

" A wee bird cam' tae oor ha' door,"
   Sang " Wae's me for Prince Charlie,"
Syne " Mary Scott " recited ower
   " The Bonnie hoose o' Airlie."

Thro' " Loudon's bonnie woods an' braes,"
   Then syne by " Bonnie Doon,"
I went gey near " Within a mile
   O' Edinburgh toon."

'Twas here I met the " White Cockade"
   Among a band o' sailors,
And " Jack o' Tar," he tripped it clean
   To the " Deil amang the tailors."

I saw " Tam Glen " an' " Duncan Gray "
   Beside the bard o' Coila ;
" Oh, Nannie wilt thou gang wi' me,"
   Said glorious Peter Baillie.

Syne " Willie brew'd a peck o' maut "
   That played us sic a plisky,
We sang gaun thro' the Cromdale Haughs
   " Neil Gow's farewell to whisky."

I then gaed ower " Glenorchy's Hills,"
   Then doon by " Craigilea,"
And danced a hoolikin aneath
   The bonnie " Rowan Tree."

" Schottiches " were the " Sodger's Joy,"
   A " Highland Reel " stood sentry,
The " Haymakers " and " Riflemen "
   Tried hard to " Keep the country."

But when the bugles a' sang truce,
   " Scotland Yet " cried never ;
Then " Triumph " sang " God save the Queen "
   And " Scotland for ever."

 left " The bush aboon Traquair "
   To see the sweet " Lochaber,"
For " A' the airts the wind can blaw,"
   There's nought like " Highland heather."

I saw the " Edinburgh Flowers ;"
   Quo' " Johnny Cope " they're plain,
" The lass o' Ballochmyle" shook hands
   Wi' " Jessie o' Dunblane."

The auld " Laird o' Cockpen " proposed
   The health o' " Annie Laurie ;"
" The lass o' Gowrie " sang fu' sweet
   " The Dowie Dens o' Yarrow."

'T was here I first " Miss Fraser " met
  From " Lovat's bonnie brae,"
Quo' I, " Gin ye will gang wi' me,"
  " By Claudie's stream we'll stray."

She sank within my arms and cried,
  " Your dearie I will be,"
Gang " Doon the burn, Davie lad,"
  And I shall " Follow thee."

Autumn.

Again the seared leaf's on the tree,
The tint so beautiful to see,
Pencilled by artistic nature;
Master touches grace each feature.
What painter e'er could mix the paint
To shade like thine, however faint;
What artist's eye, however smart,
Could imitate thy weakest part?

The golden grain on harvest field,
A precious load doth plenty yield,
Abundant food for man and beast;
Of richest mercies not the least.
Sweet, glorious autumn, mellow, wan,
In thee we see the life of man;
Youth, manhood, old age, and decay,
Like thee we come to pass away.

A Mother's Love.

Nae words o' mine can e'er lay bare
The sweetness o' a mother's care.
The fulness o' a mother's love
Is only found in Heaven above.

When we are sick an' racked wi' pain,
Her face brings aye relief again.
She kens oor tempers a' sae weel,
Nae drugs are like a mother's skeel.

She watches by oor sick bedside;
Puir body, tears she fain wad hide
Come trickling softly doon her cheek,
Foreboding fears she canna speak.

When, through her anxious, eident care,
We're able to come doon the stair,
How bright she is, joy 's in her e'e—
Thank God, my bairn is spared to me.

A mother may a favourite hae
When a' are healthy, weel, an' gay;
When trouble comes, when death is near,
The bairns are a' to her 'like dear.

How often can a thocht o' hame
A sinfu' life frae vice reclaim:
A mother's voice is heard again;
Her teaching has not been in vain

A Faded Rose.

A faded rose, withered it lay,
  With all its sweetness fled,
A beauty that once hung so gay
  Over its thorny bed.
Lovely it grew on slender stem,
  Pure as the virgin snow,
Treasured now as a priceless gem
  Of the sweet long ago.

Though time hath mixed the jet black hair,
  And age the frame hath wrung,
Remembrance comes with visions fair,
  And all again is young.
Beautiful yet, as 't was yon hour
  When joy o'erflowed the brim;
Love is an everlasting flower
  Whose eye time cannot dim.

James Beattie.
AUTHOR OF "THE MINSTREL."

Sweet minstrel bard, king of the rural scene
  Where wild flowers grow, and warbling songsters
    sing

With lusty pipe that makes the woodlands ring,
Dear to thy heart were all those scenes, I ween ;
Love at first sight, as true love aye has been,
   Thy matchless muse in harmony took wing ;
   Rich was the spoil the spoilers home did bring ;
Thy faultless ear, so exquisitely keen,
   So ill to please, divorced the bastard rhyme,
   Simplicity gave richness to the line,
While dignity and grace—the lovely pair—
   Watched o'er thy verse with vigilance sublime,
   And wheresoe'er the gems of song doth shine
The charming muse of Beattie shall be there.

The Muse.

Sweet Ettrick vale, flow on, thou gentle stream,
   Companion of my early musing years,
   When rosy hopes were tarnished with sad fears,
Lest all my joys were an ignoble dream,
Spoiling the hours in vain to catch the gleam
   Of hidden sense that ravishes the ears
   With sparkling wit, with merriment, with tears ;
Such is the gift. Alas, that mine should seem
   Unrich in thought, inelegant in line ;
   And yet, methinks, I were a traitor knave
Did I renounce the choicest gift of Heaven.
   Away, base thought. Applause is no real sign
Of worth: snug in oblivion's murky grave
Lie many lives to whom much praise was given.

Lines to a Looking-Glass.

True to all who pass thee by,
Thou wert never known to lie.
Though the tongue of mortal slips,
Truth is ever on thy lips.

Men may lie and men may swear
Falsely for the love of gear;
Thou art of an honest tribe,
Worlds could not thy honour bribe.

Thou dost show the lovely bride
In perfection's loyal pride,
While, alas! the face so plain
Sees its counterpart again.

How extensive is thy rule—
King and noble, knave and fool,
All to thee obeisance pay—
Universal is thy sway.

Hung in lofty palace hall,
Seen on humblest cottage wall;
Matron, maiden, man, and boy,
Find in thee a thing of joy.

When the youth begins to shave;
He becomes thy abject slave;
Anxiously thy face he scans,
To improve his looks he plans.

Sons of science loudly call,
Theories are put to the wall.
Empires stand and empires fall,
Yet thou shalt outlive them all.

The Armenian Massacres.

Will Britain draw the sword, or will she not ?
That is the question waiting answer now ;
Concert of Europe !—'t is a hollow sham ;
Humanity outraged demands redress
For murdered mothers, and the sweeter babe
Tossed on the cruel steel.   Will none arise
In rightful wrath to stem the crimson flow ?
Call it not war—'t is but a Christian deed
To free the slave and break the tyrant's power.
Oh ! mighty Britain ! Armenia looks to thee
With tearful eyes ; turn not thy face away ;
Right on our side, what nation need we fear ?
Success shall smile on our triumphant cause,
And despots feel the vengeance of their crimes.

A Scotch Tribute to William Watson.

Most noble bard, I early loved thy song,
  So daint'ly phrased and exquisitely turned,
  Where rich and sweet poetic fancy burned,
That heaved thy name high in the gifted throng––
Th' immortal ones.   More proud ye are among
  The noble ones who have compassion learned
  For human woes, and cruelty have spurned.
Can ever war be either bad or wrong
Waged in the cause of precious liberty?
  Well done, sweet bard, thy fame shall never die
The persecuted in yon Eastern land
Shall bless thy name in holy fervency.
  Great thy reward, if not on earth, on high
At Heaven's bar, where all shall one day stand.

The Snowdrop.

Pure snowdrop, first of Flora's train
  To brave the wintry spring,
Brief herald of the leafless plain,
  What tidings dost thou bring?

Thou hast survived the blighting east,
  The deadness of the year,
Appearing, when expected least,
  The heart of man to cheer.

When other gems beneath the clod
    Unconscious slumbering lie,
Thy snowy bosom breasts the sod
    The earth to glorify.

Thou com'st when earth is bleak and bare,
    A miracle of God,
Sufficient to dissolve in air
    The sceptic and his code.

Thou bring'st a message from the dead,
    An echo from the grave—
The soul shall incorruption wed,
    And life immortal have.

When sad with grief, harassed with care,
    Our hearts with sorrow blent,
We note thy meek, submissive air,
    And learn to be content.

Wee Jim.

He cam oor ingle side to grace,
A bonny bairn wi' chubby face,
And een sae innocent and blue
               Had little Jim.
His mother's pet, the laddie grew
               A roguish limb.

C

He creepit, then began to walk,
An' syne wi' faither raised the crack ;
He askit quastions unco deep
                      On subjects dim ;
I had to lay my brains asteep
                      To answer him.

He thrave an' grew a sturdy loon,
The foremost laddie in the toon ;
When fechts took place Jim aye was there
                      Withooten doot,
To see that justice fair an' square
                      Was ladled oot.

The lad was clever, smert, an' gleg ;
His mother spae'd a future big
Wi' hope, that he micht some day reach
                      The tapmaist bough ;
Or in a poopit stand an' preach,
                      And wag his pow.

But daith cam.   'Tis the human lot,
And wee Jim left the family cot
For faulds mair bieldy, where the lambs
                      Are safe wi' Him
Whose gentle voice the storm calms
                      To shelter them.

Lord Dalkeith's Marriage.

From Liddesdale to sweet Bowhill,
  Drumlanrig to Clydeside,
All wish prosperity, goodwill
  To Dalkeith and his bride.

Our hearts with love are flowing wide
  Upon this bridal morn ;
May health and joy on every side
  Their future home adorn !

May smiling fortune, rosy, bright,
  With flowers their path bestrew,
And every gift with love unite
  To bless the House Buccleuch !

The clanship feeling still persists
  To live in Ettrick's core ;
The love of chieftain still exists
  Strong 's in the days of yore,

When bold Buccleuch of memory green
  To Willie's * rescue flew,
And taught Elizabeth, I ween,
  What brave men dared to do.

O may it ever be our lot
  To have a Dalkeith true—
Heir to the noble line of Scott,
  The Ducal House Buccleuch.

          * Kinmont Willie.

In Memoriam—W. Dalgleish, Potburn.

Bring me a bunch of violets wild
   From the burnside where the primrose grows,
To lay on the grave of the youthful bard
   That lived and died where the Ettrick flows.

Bring me a lily, pure and white,
   And a sweet moss rose of freshest bloom,
With a heather sprig from his native hills—
   Most royal wreath for a poet's tomb.

Bring me a bit of yellow broom,
   And a blossom'd twig of hawthorn spray ;
I lovingly gaze on his favourite flowers,
   And sadly repeat his sweetest lay.

Unstring the harp.   The singer sleeps
   'Neath Ettrick Pen, where the wild wind blows;
The turmoil of life he hath left behind
   For the grave's serene and calm repose.

In Memoriam—Doctor Shaw.

An old familiar form is gone,
   A face we loved to see,
While Yarrow's hills still gaze upon
   Life's mortal destiny.

No more shall Yarrow's stream serene,
　　Nor solitary dell
By lone St Mary's, wild Loch Skene,
　　Which tourists haunt so well,

Behold the man who laughed to scorn
　　The wildest winter day,
As staff in hand at early morn
　　He trudged his weary way ;

That racking pain he might relieve—
　　And I have heard him say
Although no fee he did receive,
　　True thanks were ample pay.

With cunning hand and judgment sound,
　　By either night or day,
The efficacious drug he found
　　That charmed disease away.

The healing art, I am assured,
　　Hath lost a clever son,
Whose modesty would fain obscured
　　The triumphs he had won.

So kindly by the fever bed
　　For hours he would attend,
And oft remained while others fled—
　　The sympathising friend.

Yes, he had faults, but who has not?
  He who is best may say;
But time shall cherish a green spot
  For him that is away.

Sonnet—Treachery.

Treachery, the most odious crime in
All the catalogue of human vices.
I can forgive a multitude of faults,
I can overlook innumerable
Failings. All men are liable to err.
All have come far short of being perfect.
I can forgive almost every crime, but
Foul treachery is unpardonable.
That man is a reptile in human shape
Who, under the mean disguise of friendship,
Works upon the feelings of his friend, till
He has gained his confidence, then betrays
Him at the first opportunity. I
Shun that man as I would a pestilence—
Contamination is in his touch. His
Breath's more poisonous than the deadly plague.
That man's soul, I say, is lost to honour;
He knows nothing of the dignity of
Man. His life is but a living falsehood.

With him self-respect has no connection.
Give me a man on whom I can depend,
Yea, even though he had a thousand faults,
This one virtue redeems them all.   Whose pulse
Beats steady as the stroke of the piston
Of a well-regulated engine.   Vice
Has its degrees of wickedness, even
As virtue has degrees of excellence ;
But of all the devilish inventions, whose
Evils have for six thousand years harassed
A world, and whose discovery alone
Rests with responsible men, treachery
For pure rank villainy appals them all.

A Mither's Sang.

DEDICATED TO "SURFACEMAN."

My bairnies sweet, I will sing a sang
  Wi' a tune ye like to hear ;
I 'll lilt it ower i' the Scottish tongue
  That 's sae pleasin' to the ear.

I 'll sing it wi' a' a mither's pride,
  Tho' the heart's dew dims my e'e,
Thinking when ye shall be scattered wide
  Frae the dear auld hame an' me.

There 's Tam, when he 's grown to be a man,
  Like his faither strong an' brave,
The battle o' life he 'll nobly plan
  An' fecht it among the lave.

Wee Rab, the loon wi' the cunning e'e—
  Wha kens what he yet may dae ?
Wha kens but he yet may tap the tree
  An' the formaist fiddle play ?

An' Jim, wi' the bonny curly heid,
  Wha sleeps at the wa' sae soun',
Has maybe dreams o' the Muse's glead
  O' the poet's sweetest croon.

An' Jenny, nae higher thochts for you
  Ever come within my mind,
Than you be a woman kind and true,
  An' to virtue's path inclined.

Noo, bairnies, strip, an' your prayers say
  Ere ye cuddle doon for the nicht ;
An' God shall protect you on life's way
  If ye always do the richt.

Summer.

Now summer comes clad in a wreath of flowers,
    And beauty decks the bonny woodland bowers,
Where lovers sit and whisper future joys,
    When love shall gild the ever cloudless skies.

The spreading beech o'erlaps the peaceful scene,
    The primrose stars add glory to the green ;
Sweet whistling birds from every twig and spray
    More charming make the gladsome summer day.

Now softer winds from off the sunny south
    Blow pleasantly to nurse the tender youth ;
The summer skies spread out a sheet of blue,
    And warmer suns dispel the early dew.

Gay summer, gayest of the seasons all,
    How soft and light thy airy footsteps fall ;
We hail with joy the time when thou dost send
    Thy gifts abroad to beautify our land.

Sonnet—Hope.

The human mind is a garden, wherein
Flowers and weeds intermingled grow ;
Water'd by faith the tender buds spring forth,
Their nourishment drawn from the healthy vein
Of love. They flourish and abound in joy,

Yet hope is the gardener, by whose aid
The reward is made sure.   Man's existence
On earth were but a punishment unless
Hope brightened the prospects of the future.
The working man hopes some day to be rich,
The rich man hopes he may be richer still,
The maiden hopes to wed the man she loves.
Life is thus sweeten'd at no one's expense ;
All the energies of the human mind
Are roused to action.   Life is ennobled,
The sharp spur of victory is driven home
Into the jaded ribs of idleness.
Hopeful of success, efforts are renewed
With redoubled fury, the pulse beats high,
Every nerve vibrates strong under the strain.
Daily toil becomes indeed a pleasure,
The proud belted earl is not envied.   Why?
The ploughman with hope is as rich as he.
Happiness is not measured by wealth, nor
Is contentment always the rich man's friend.
A good conscience is a safe companion ;
Thrice happy the man who has possession
Of such a treasure.   That man is a king.
Hope worketh thus as a strong medicine
To keep the machinery in order,
Else one part did not do its duty to
Correspond harmoniously with the
Working of another part.   Hope kills the
Rust of laziness, polishes afresh
Those glorious jewels, heart, soul, and mind.

Sonnet—Love:

Love, the sweetest word in all our language,
  No word can give a right definition,
Or a true meaning of that one word love ;
  In the dictionary it stands unique,
Sweetest spring of all in the human breast,
  Thy waters are ever pure ; thy fountain,
The heart, is never tainted with passions—
  Those bitters that disgrace humanity.
Thy very name is amply sufficient
  To recommend without certificate
The beautiful queen of all the graces,
  Thy string is never discordant.   Never
Harsh the tone of thy sweet musical lyre,
  Peace and joy are thy bosom comrades, life
Is blest by thy hallowing influence.
  The coy maid acting under thy potent
Spell, gives her heart away once and for all,
  Henceforth she lives for another ; those sweet
Eyes unconsciously divulge her secret ;
  On her cheek the rose and lily play at
Hide and seek ; the least sound startles her, the
  Voice of her darling is the sweetest sound
She ever heard ; yes, she is supremely
  Happy.   Oh, who that has ever tasted
Truly of the fresh waters of first love
  Ever drinks with the same relish again.
What power cannot do, love can accomplish ;
  Is there a task too hard for love to do ?

Love melts the treacherous ice of friendship,
 Love is the most potent power in the world.
In all her dealings she hath no revenge.
 Through love we live, move, and have our being ;
Through love we are happy now, and through love
 A glorious hereafter is made sure.

———

Sonnet—Liberty.

How grand and great a boon is liberty ;
No freeman knows the value of it.   Why ?
Because he never knew the want of it.
Ask the slave what freedom means ; will he be
Able to tell you ?   Ah, I guess he will.
Goaded to death by a hard taskmaster ;
The loaded whip his daily companion ;
Would he not have sense enough to know that
Liberty meant redemption from all his
Hardships, and elevation to comfort ?
It were madness to imagine ought else.
How glorious is the privilege that
We free born Britons enjoy !   We can walk
Abroad on this beautiful earth of ours,
And meditate on all the beauties of
Creation ; we hear the birds singing their
Morning hymn of praise ; we see the fragrant
Flowers unfolding their sweetness every hour,

And worshipping the God that made them in
Silent adoration ; we see the snow
In winter in its unapproachable
Whiteness, covering the earth in beauty ;
We see the spring emerging from the womb,
Diffusing a glorious animation
On all the land.   Can we see all this and
Be insensible to the blessings we
Daily enjoy, compared with the lot of
Others ?   Oh, may my soul be stirred within
Me to give thanks to the Great Author of
Them all !   Freedom, what a blessing thou art ;
The tongue of man is inadequate to
Name thy joys ; thou feed'st the heart with sweetest
Nurture ; the springs of life, when poisoned with
Oppression, regain their elasticity
At the sacred fountain of liberty.
Liberty and health, twin sisters of joy,
What more doth a man require than them
To live ; yea, to live wisely, pure, and well.

Sonnet—Health.

Oh, how glorious is youthful manhood
In all the vigour of its juicy prime ;
Oh, weak, puny man stretched on the bed of
Sickness, torn with agonising pain, when
Thou wert in health thou thought'st lightly of it.

What wouldst thou not give to be strong again?
Worlds if thou hadst them to give were too small
An offering to give in exchange for health.
Yet worlds cannot buy it.   Young man, wilt thou
Take advice?   No, thou art too conceited;
"Let me alone," cries the worldling; "I know
Well enough without any intermeddling
How to govern my life.   Stand back; what right
     have
You to interfere with me and disturb
My enjoyments?"   Oh, young man, I would plead
With thee, despise not the voice of wisdom;
Thou hast no wish to die before thy time—
Life is sweet to you, to me, and all God's
Creatures.   To die is the last of our thoughts,
But die we must.   Clay must to clay return.
But abuse not the greatest gift which an
All-wise and merciful Creator in
His infinite wisdom and goodness hath
Bestowed on man.   Once more I say "Take care;"
I know well enough the fascinating
Allurements of youth; I have been young
Myself; I've no wish to judge you harshly.
Set your compass at sobriety, and
See that the needle remains undisturbed;
Be temperate in all thy enjoyments,
Lest Nature, outraged, shall have her revenge.
See yon young man in the full flush of health—
Strong is the muscle of his brawny arm,
Bright is the sparkle of his clear blue eye,

The stethoscope gives no indication
Of danger to the practised ear.   Why?
Health is delineated on every
Feature; doctors' drugs have no charm for him.
The beauty of a young man is his strength.
The favours of kings, what are they?   Trifles.
Oh, earth, thou hast no blessing like good health.

In Memoriam—Gough.

The great apostle of temperance is
No more.   If a grateful nation showers its
Laurels upon the man expert in war,
What honours are too great for the man whose
Highest aim is the people's good?   Gough was
A hero.   A hero, did I say?   Yea,
He was something more.   He was a hero
Of heroes.   His message to men was peace.
And how did he fulfil it?   Nobly.   Oh,
How nobly did he plead the cause he had
So much at·heart; his eloquence carried
The barbed arrows of conviction home, and
Thousands were redeemed from slavery.
He sleeps now; but we grudge him not his rest.
He is gone; but he has left behind him
The richest of legacies—a good name.

First Love.

Can a man forget his first and early
Love? Can the sweet dream of youth be consigned
To oblivion? Can that sweet passion that
Awoke in his breast all that was sweetly
Human, and made him a man in spite of
Himself, be remembered no more? Never.
Oh, never, can the violet eyes of her
Who first taught me the way to love, lose their
Sweetness. Neither can their wistful gaze
Ever be effaced from my memory.
That look that told me so much can never
Die. 'T is photographed for eternity.
Long years have rolled by since I bade my first
Love adieu. With glistening eyes we parted.
Henceforth from that day life lost its brightness.
But why speak I of it? 'T were treason to
Lift the veil even for a moment. To
Me she is as sweet and dear as that hour
We first embraced. Tell me not, for I will
Not believe it, that first love is a boy's
Delusion. Go and whisper it to the
Babbling crowd, who know no better, but stand
Back from me, for I scorn your doctrine. It
Is poison to my soul.
And what a small thing separates lovers!
A lover's quarrel can be healed, but the
Wound leaves a mark. There is a grief
That mars the joy even in its happiest hours.

Truth.

The great enemy of the human race
Is a miserable, malicious lie.
Aye speak the truth, the honest, naked truth.
Who can estimate the priceless value
Of a pure conscience, void of all offence?
Integrity's the mainspring of manhood.
As the safety of a ship depends on
The ability of the commander,
So does the happiness of human life
On the principle that rules its actions.
Sow tares, and thou shalt reap accordingly.
Where is the man that has not sense enough
To know that the making or marring of
His life, either for here or hereafter,
Is entrusted to no one but himself?
Look well, O man, that thou judgest wisely;
Load not thy understanding with theories.
One good deed nobly and faithfully done
'S worth more than a thousand good intentions
Promised; plann'd often, but never fulfilled.
How beautiful a thing it is to speak
The truth! Truth makes man more noble still.
Vow not at all if thou canst not perform.
I would rather be called a coward than
A liar. The shafts of envy cannot
Damage the cause of truth. Triumphantly
It stands secure amidst a host of foes.

D

Sonnet—True Love.

True love comes only once in a lifetime:
Men and women may have passing fancies,
But call them not by the sweet name of love.
Have I aught to gain by telling lies?   No,
But a great deal to lose.   Hear, then, the truth;
I am regardless of contradiction;
I care neither for the praise of men nor
The scoffing jeers of a sceptical world.
The poet who at some great lordling's feet
Would bow and cringe for favour is a slave,
Even to himself, and is unworthy
The name of bard.   I pity the poor wretch
Who for patronage prostitutes his muse—
God's noblest gift to man.   Yet there are such
Who speak not truth because it might offend.
Flattery, how detestable thou art,
With thy oily tongue and honey'd phrases!
Deception your daily occupation,
You become an adept at deceiving.
But thou shalt not cheat me, thou base villain;
I shall clip thy tongue with the shears of truth,
And close crop thy ears with the hedge-knife of
Justice.   Think'st thou I am not in earnest?
Begone, mean hound, else my furious muse
Lash thy dirty carcase to within an
Inch of thy life.   Are there more loves than one?
There is but only one true, perfect love;
He or she who loves once never loves more,

Because they have no love to give.   The fire
That once so sweetly glowed in the furnace
Of the heart has consumed all the fuel;
There is nothing left but sacred ashes
Inurned in the cemetery of the mind,
Never more to be rekindled this side
The grave.   Oh, how sweet is the sensation
We feel when under the spell of first love.
To the man intoxicated with love
Adam has never fallen; he sees nothing
But beauty, glorious beauty, around him;
He hears not the harsh sounds of a busy
World; earth is a perfect elysium—
He is virtually in Paradise.

My First Run.

The dying sun shone sweet and cool,
The ripplets danced upon the pool
Below the Loup; * the fishers gay
Had plied their rods the lee lang day
Without success; when, lo, a scream—
" He's hook't 'im " ran along the stream.
The talking groups forgot their theme,
The creed of politics was tame
To sport like this.   With trembling hand
I deftly held my lancewood wand;

* A famous salmon rest in Ettrick.

Large drops of sweat broke o'er my brow,
My heart beat as 't would beat right through.
Each looker-on, with anxious face,
Gave good advice, with serious grace,
How I should act.   The mighty fish
Wheeled madly with a sudden splash,
And cleft the waters with a dash
That made the foam recoil.   The reel,
Upon its smooth revolving wheel,
Swiftly spun out the corded line
With regularity how fine !
The music, how it jerried on
Until the length was nearly done ;
Now back, now forward, time about,
Now winding up, now plying out.
The final struggle now began,
Which proves the science of the man.
Steady, now came the tug of war,
Wild in its course as comet star,
Fleet as the racehorse on the plain,
Or gallant ship upon the main,
It ploughed the stream with furious strife
In its grand and noble race for life.
Checked in its wild career, the pain
Of the otter'd hook made more plain
By the sure, steady, constant strain
Of the trusty line, the great fish
Gave a plunge, then a sullen splash,
And all was o'er.   Worn out it lay
With side upturned upon the spray.

" Wind up now gently for the side,
I'll land 'im for you," some one cried ;
With napkin firm rolled round his hand,
A splendid fish lay on dry land,
Amid loud cheers of " Grandly done,"
Cheers that proclaimed my spurs were won,
I finished my first salmon run.

Sonnet—Pride.

Of all the privileged evils that disgrace
Society, pride is by far the worst.
What care I for the monied millionaire,
With his purse-proud looks and lofty bearing ?
Nature has been as kind to me as him ;
He, like myself, is only mortal.   Chance
Or fortune may have lined his pouches with
Yellow sovereigns, and mine with poverty,
But what of that ?   The fountain of honour
Springs not from titles, neither hath virtue
Her dwelling exclusively in mammon.
She is as bright an ornament in the
Cottage hall as in the royal palace.
I detest pride above every evil;
Allied with poverty 't is disgusting.
'T is a canker worm in the human heart,

Eating the beauty out of our nature
By its selfish abominableness.
A poor earth worm puff'd up with pride is as
Sorrowful a sight as can be witnessed.
The narrow mansion destined for his couch
Knows no respect of persons.   Vanity
Of vanities, the mind is still the man.
I may lose good opportunities of
Worldly advancement by being too frank
With my opinions.   Well, let it be so.
'T is my choice, and my conscience is my own.
I would not touch my hat in passing, and
Say good morning, sir, to a gentleman
Because a coronet adorn'd his brow.
I do it out of respect for the man,
And not the coat he wears.   Gold is useful,
But love can procure what wealth ne'er could buy.
I would not have people to make themselves
Too cheap.   I love to see a nice sense of
Honour, and a judicious self-esteem.
Independence is good, but, my brother
And sister, there is a happy medium.
Exalt not thyself, O man, for the proud
Shall be brought low, and the haughty humbled.
A little pride will do no harm, but see
That you make it the handmaid of prudence.

Sonnet—War.

War! what a dire calamity thou art,
The curse of nations and the sport of kings;
The cruel bayonet stabs, the sabre cleaves,
The thundering cannon spews its deadly hail,
Men fall like leaves on a frosty morning.
The fountains of blood are opened, and the
Earth is steeped with that rich element that
Constitutes the life of man.   The battle-
Field presents a sickening sight, the groans of
The dying, the fierce agonies of the
Wounded, as if all the fiends of hell were
Let loose at once.   And this is " glory !"
Peaceful hamlets are ransacked and plundered,
The useful art of husbandry is checked,
The fruitful fields are turned into a vast
Sea of carnage.   Oh, infernal war, how
Bloody are thy evils !   The widow mourns
The loss of a darling husband, and the
Sweet infant prattling at its mother's knee,
By one cruel stroke, is orphaned for life.
The modest maid whose gallant lover is
A lodger in the tented field, knows well
That she has to depend on the chance of
War for the consummation of that bliss
Which shall complete her earthly happiness.
Oh, that nations would live in harmony !

Oh, for that good time when man shall clasp the
Hand of brother man, and peace, glorious
Peace, reign omnipotent o'er all the earth,
When every man shall sit under his own
Fig tree, none daring to make him afraid !

Sonnet—Sincerity.

Oh, for the good name of an honest man !
That man is a hero, braver far than
He who risks his life at the cannon's mouth,
Honours more great than all the spoils of war,
Laurels more bright than e'en the victor's crown
Are his by right.   Creation's noblest work.
Whose soul abhors a base and shameful lie,
Whose every word 's as binding as his bond ;
That man wields a power kings sigh for in vain.
To see him is only but to love him,
To know him is only but to trust him.
I would not give two straws for that man
Who would argue an opinion which he
Knew was false, opposed to principle and
Reason, which even hardened conscience
Did righteously condemn.   Give me a man
Who will sternly stand to his convictions
Truthfully, without either fear or favour ;
Whose structure is built on solid justice,

Not animated by fierce contention ;
Not arguing just for argument's sake,
But to aid the cause of glorious truth.
Sincerity, how glorious is thy fame !
As firm and enduring as time itself,
Thou shalt withstand the decay of ages.
Empires may totter, crumble into dust,
And be but things of the past.   Mighty time,
The remorseless destroyer, may do this;
Yet thou shalt remain triumphant, and shine
Brilliant as the beautiful stars of heaven
That crown the glory of the Milky Way.

Sonnet—Learning.

How eloquent is the man of learning ;
He is an intellectual giant :
That man towers far above the man whose speech
Is unadorned.   There is no royal road
To the palatial mansion of wisdom,
Wherein dwells that priceless jewel, knowledge.
The ladder is steep and ill to climb, but
When once the top is reached, how sweet the joy
The climber feels that now his toils are o'er.
The traveller on the desert plain feels all
The pangs of thirst.   Wearied, still plodding on,
He gains the spring that cools his thirsty soul,

And rests awhile; then with renewed strength
He starts refreshed, and safely wins the goal.
Oh, glorious knowledge, how excellent are
All thy pleasant fruits, how sweet thy dainties,
Yet thricely bitter if they are abused.
Far better never to have known at all
Than know and do the sin, however small.
Experience is the great boarding school,
Wherein wisdom is taught, but the school fees
Are heavy, and gold may be bought too dear;
Still the knowledge that is bought hath greater
Value in the purchaser's eyes than that
Instruction which can be got for nothing,
And with which the market is overstocked.
When a boy at school, what a hardship I
Thought it was to learn my task; suffice be
It to say since then I have had ample
Opportunities for discovering
The huge mistake I made.   Regret is vain—
I lost the chance that never comes again.

The Storm, 1895.

The Ice King reigns on his mighty throne,
    Majestic, strong as a king should be;
The snow lies deep, while the suffering poor
    Are hungering sore in their poverty.

The rich man sits in his cosy room,
 Surveys the frost with a cheerful eye;
He always knows of a well-cooked meal,
 It matters not how the snowflakes fly.

The sharp-teethed wind from the surly east,
 That cuts through the garment thin and bare,
He feels it not, for the fur-lined coat
 Can foil with ease the assailing air.

I don't believe in the catching theme,
 So deftly taught by mistaken men,
Of equal rights, and a common purse—
 Each night would see a "divide" again.

But I sometimes think of the man of wealth,
 And what laurels bright he might have won,
For one day he'll find, to his heavy cost,
 He did not do what he should have done.

The poor must live, and the time is now
 When human love should be freely given;
If the deed brings no reward on earth,
 It shall be richly repaid in heaven.

The Auld Fireside.

What changes hae ta'en place wi' a',
   Changes far-reaching, wide,
Since youth upon us lichtly sat
When we were bonnie bairnies at
   The auld fireside.

When prayers a' were duly said,
   With what affection, pride,
Sweet mother kissed each darlin' babe,
And laid us snugly in oor crib
   'Yont the fireside.

She bade us hae a fear o' guid,
   And in the Lord confide,
And we would never gang astray,
Though time might take us far away
   From the fireside.

Baith faither, mother, noo are gane
   To swell the unseen tide:
Life's battles we have had to fight,
Smoothed by the halo of the light
   O' yon fireside.

Though we hae hames noo o' oor ain,
   A dear wife by oor side,
And other happiness we 've found,
Nae joys can be the joys around
   The auld fireside.

Only an Orphan Boy.

Be kind to the laddie that comes to your door,
Barefit an' raggit an' wandering his lane;
And gi'e him a piece frae your weel plenished store,
Wha filled your meal ark can renew it again.

Turn not on your heel wi' a jibe an' a sneer,
Be gentle and tender, 't will soften his care;
In doing so an angel some day may appear,
Perhaps entertain one an' not be aware.

Ye ken na yoursel' what yer ain yet may need,
Ye ken na the road yer ain yet may gang;
Oh, dinna be saucy an toss up yer heid,
'T is often the best that gang aye farest wrang.

To him the sweet name o' a kind mother dear,
The comforts and sweets o' a cosy wee hame,
Is a language unkenned to the puir laddie's ear:
He's heard o' sic things, but he never knew them.

Oh, wha could be harsh to a bonnie wee bairn?
Oh, wha to its cry could e'er turn a deaf ear?
Yet some hae a heart that is caulder than airn,
And self is the god that they worship sincere.

Let us be freendly ilk ane to each other,
Let's help aye oor neebor as far as we can;
The lowest an' meanest is still aye my brother,
He's stamped wi' the image and likeness o' man.

Remember that God a' oor actions does see,
Wha lends to the Lord never lendeth in vain ;
And think o' the joys that kind sympathies gi'e
To the heart that 's forlorn and aching wi' pain.

Let oor actions be just, oor intentions sincere,
Let us always dae richt though the crowd may dae
      wrang ;
And at last we 'll know joys that are purer, more dear,
And sing a far sweeter and holier sang.

In Memory of the Authoress of the Song— "The March of the Cameron Men."

Another sweet singer has crossed that bourne
From whence no traveller returns.   Gifted
As she highly was with the voice of song,
She has left behind her at least one which
Cannot die—"The March of the Cameron Men."
We mourn for the irreparable loss ;
Poesy weeps o'er her honoured daughter's
Bier.   Yet we are happy in the thought that
She has left earth's bliss for joys more refined ;
That now a brighter crown than earth could give
Adorns her lovely brow, that she now sings
A sweeter song than ever she did here.

In Memoriam — Lord Randolph Churchill.

Another gap.   Brave Randolph 's now no more—
As brave a man as ever mother bore ;
And England mourns a son she proudly loved.
No statesman's death for many, many years
Has drawn forth such multitudes of tears
From high and low.   A nation's heart is moved.

In joy we watched the brilliant life begun ;
We saw it close before the prize was won,
Yet much is left that history shall pen.
By accident of birth, a noble lord,
His gifts were such as amply could afford
To scorn that rank that ne'er ennobles men.

So noble, young !   We think what might have been,
So possible ; and yet, methinks, I ween
Death takes no bribe, not even from the throne.
'T was not to be.   How vain it is to plan
The future out, and which no mortal can
U naided ever build.   Churchill is gone !

Weep Not.

The balmy days of autumn's past,
The sky-blue hours of summer's lost,
　　And spring so sweet to see.
Now swirling leaves, a mighty host,
Decayed 'neath winter's hoary frost,
　　Sweep o'er the frozen lea—
　　　　To take me home,
　　　　Now winter's come,
　　With a snowy shroud for me.

The pains that in my bosom burn,
The sleepless nights till dawning morn
　　In the watches all alone,
Proclaim that Death, the giant king,
Hath struck the last, the fatal sting.
　　My sands of life are run;
　　　　Methinks I hear,
　　　　In accents clear,
　　A sweet voice saying "Come."

No more to me shall spring come back
With those bright flowers I used to deck
　　My little sister's hair;
When round the fire on winter night
The family meet, my spirit bright
　　Shall haunt my empty chair—
　　　　Though distant far,
　　　　Yet closely near,
　　In the vacant space of air.

Weep not for me, thine only son,
Mourn not that death's so early come
   To break the family chain;
My wearied soul flies to the rest,
Like a dove that's wandered from the nest,
   And homeward turns again;
      No more to stray,
      But ever stay
   In Heaven's blest domain.

The Lover's Lament.

And now must you leave me, sweet Annie, for ever?
And thou, cruel Death, oh, why should you sever
   Hearts that so loving entwine?
Thou art going, sweet maid, to the land of the blest,
To slumber in peace on thy Saviour's breast,
   Where glorified mortals shine,
     Where endless day
     Doth last for aye
   In those glorious realms divine.

My love, to the grave thou art hastening fast,
Like an autumn leaf 'neath the winter blast,
   Or a sheaf of ripe, ripe corn.

E

The hand of Death is upon thee, love,
While angels wait to escort above
  Thy soul to eternal morn,
    Where spirits bright
    In floods of light
  The heavenly land adorn.

Thy life was pure as the virgin snow,
Thou wast far too good for this vale of woe,
  With its sorrows, sins, and tears;
Like a flower that hath newly shed its bloom,
But ere night hath come its sweet perfume
  In the low, low earth appears,
    A blossom'd stem,
    A broken gem,
  Which an injured beauty wears.

But one request I ask, sweet love,
From the spirit-land of saints above—
  That you be my guiding star;
In the silent watches of the night
May thy holy will in radiance bright
  E'en condescend so far
    To urge me on
    To gain that home
  In which we part no more.

I would fain you had lived to be my bride,
For thou wast aye my joy, my pride,

And how kind thou used to be
When aye we met at the trysting place ;
And how tender was the sweet embrace
When I parted, love, from you ;   ·
 'T was but a dream,
 For it would seem
It had never been to be.

To the Memory of Mark Akenside, Poet.

Green be the laurels round thy brow :
The honours bright thou well hast won.
Like snawdraps on the grassy knowe—
Like bonnie rosebuds all alone—
Conspicuous thy genius shown,
 In dazzling, bright array,
  Sweet Akenside !

The glories of the darling muse
Illumed thy clear, creative brain ;
The meanest subject thou didst choose
In beauty's robes was clothed again :
Like showers of calm refreshing rain
 Thou paintedst Nature gay,
  Sweet Akenside !

Thy name immortal ne'er shall die,
Thy splendid fame shall ever live :
Like the pure orbs in yon blue sky
Thy lines the heart can always move,
So sweet, pathetic is thy love,
  Thy tender graceful way,
    Sweet Akenside !

Spring weeps because thou 'rt now no more,
Summer mourns o'er thy cherished grave ;
E'en rueful Autumn murmurs sore,
And maniac Winter wild doth rave :
While o'er thy grave sweet flowerets wave,
  And silent homage pay,
    Sweet Akenside !

The wastlin' winds that breezy blaw
Ower mossy hill and bracken'd dell,
Where sleeps the canny maukin braw—
Where blooms sae grand the sweet blue bell—
Had they but tongues, their grief to tell,
  Would softly, sadly say,
    Sweet Akenside !

And other poets yet unborn
Shall glean fresh ardour at thy tomb,
And flourish like the smiling morn
Awakened newly from the womb—
Dispelling sorrow, mist, and gloom—
  In glory chant the lay,
    Sweet Akenside !

Burns' Birthday.

In seventeen hunder an' fifty-nine,
Amid a blast o' Januar' win',
   Auld Scotia's bard was born,
Within an auld, wee theekit hoose
This lad sae hamely, sweet, and douce,
   First saw the licht o' morn.
      The howdy wife
      Spaed oot the life
   The laddie wad adorn.

While yet a lad, within his breast
A patriotic love did rest
   For Scotia's bonnie isle;
While yet a lad, his blood grew hot
For every dear romantic spot
   Within the bounds o' Coil;
      Wi' love complete,
      He sang sae sweet,
   The joys o' honest toil.

Reared 'mid the humblest o' the poor,
The fragrance o' his lyric power
   Would bow its head to none;
The learned men o' every clime
Admired the sweet an' pithy rhyme
   O' Scotia's darling son.
      A brighter crown
      O' more renown
   No poet ever won.

To-night, wherever Scotsmen meet,
Dear Robbie's sangs, sae couthie, sweet,
   Are sung wi' rantin' glee;
Where Lugar flows an' Afton glides
His name immortal ever bides:
    And far across the sea
      It is the same;
      They sing o' hame
    Maybe with misty e'e.

Peace to his ashes; peace, I say,
And drop a tear above his clay,
   Wrung from a heart sincere.
Now that the bard has gone to rest,
In silence let us drink the toast
    Of him we loved so dear.
      He was our ain,
      An' ne'er again
    His equal shall appear.

June.

Sweet green-leafed June, we welcome thee
   Most fervent and sincere;
Arrayed in beauty's royal robes,
   We hail thee with a cheer.

The barren days of Spring are o'er
  With their bleak, dismal hue,
Now southern winds in playful mood
  Blow soft and cool on you.

The balmy azure sky above,
  The fresh green earth below,
Make us forget the piercing winds
  Of Winter, wreathed in snow.

Sweet clover blooms—red, yellow, white,
  Beguile the busy bee ;
The amorous buttercups have wed
  The daisies on the lea.

From every flower, from every bird,
  A welcome warm and true,
Unsparingly each hour 's bestowed
  Caressingly on you.

The corncraik, thy favourite bird,
  The ryegrass swaiths among,
Blythe wakes the sweets of evening's close
  With his pathetic song.

All nature hails thee with applause
  Sweet as the chorded tune,
The muffled winds that softly blow
  Sing ' Welcome, royal June.'

The Roarin' Game.

Heard ye the curlers at their play ?
Heard ye their lood hip, hip, hurrah ?
Heard ye the language used by them
At Scotland's truly national game ?

Ca' 'way, man, Jock, come tae ma cowe !
Ye're ower sune here, I doot 'e 're throwe ;
Couldna been better—just the spot ;
Oh, grand, man ! ask them now whae's shot.

Noo, Jamie, lad, she'll hae tae walk ;
Juist crack an egg upon her back ;
Losh, Jim, but ye hae dune it neat ;
I kenn'd she'd ne'er warm in her seat.

Noo, Dave, ye like a guid strang play ;
I carena if ye see't away—
Dave thocht a meenit, soled her nice,
And sent her spinnin' fair howe ice.

Mercy, how guid ! juist chap an' lie ;
A bonnet lyin' fair tee high—
The skip he danced, an' roared for joy—
Cried, " King o' players, tee hoie ! tee hoie "

Man, Andra, for a gaird be shure ;
Be ower the hog—losh, man, take care !
Soop, Jock ; man, soop ! man, gi' 'er the cowe !
Another pund ; stop, haud up now !

A glorious play, sae strecht an' true ;
Whae ever played a shot like you ?
A tell 'e, Andra, for a fack,
Ye fairly hae the curlin' knack.

Excitement 's keen, the hin'maist stane
Comes slidin' ower the icy plain
An' lies the shot !   Oo've won the day ;
Up wi' the cowes—hurrah ! hurrah !

Oor Youthfu' Days.

Oor youthfu' days, sic happy days,
When bairns we roved aboot the braes ;
We clam the trees and tore oor claes—
The tawse but added tae oor waes
            When we gaed hame.

We guddled in the burnie clear,
For wat feet then we had nae fear ;
Oor breek-feet oft we had to wring,
Yet durst nae tell o' sic a thing
            When we gaed hame.

We kenn'd o' nests on tree an' hag—
Wha kenn'd the maist had aye the brag ;
And when at bools we lost oor a'
Wi' knuckler on we changed the thraw,
            And wan the game.

Sic glorious days at schule we had;
For some wee lass we focht and bled,
Whose wee sweet face doon through the years
At odd times noo an' then appears
                    The same's lang syne.

And when oor spells we couldna say,
And when oor coonts we couldna dae,
We got oor licks, got keepit in,
When lett'n oot we sherp did rin
                    Away for hame.

Those happy days, like morning mist
That creeps along the mountain breast,
Hae fled before the dawning day;
We'd nocht tae care for then but play
                    When we gaed hame.

The battles noo we fecht are waur
Than when at schule we used to spar;
Temptations that we knew not then
Assail us noo—watch weel, O man,
                    And mind aye hame.

Then let us pray tae God ilk nicht
Tae guide oor fitsteps aye aricht,
Oor actions aye fair honour bricht,
Then joyously we'll wing oor flicht
                    Tae oor last hame.

Love's First Dawn.

First love, O tell me not it is a dream,
Painting the dawn of manhood ; like a gleam
Of dying sunset, noble, pure, and fair ;
Leaving no mark to tell it once was there.

'T is vain to think that we can clear the mind
Of joys, on which fond memory oft hath dined,
Nor made the banquet less ; time but supplies
A double charm to love that never dies.

My queen of hearts, I love to think of thee—
What thou hast been and all thou didst for me,
When fiery blood and youthful follies reigned ;
The thought of thee my wayward steps restrained.

Those glorious eyes that made me walk on air,
I see them now—they haunt me everywhere ;
Yet sweeter far those ruby lips that told
A tale of love too sacred to unfold.

Though destined not to have thee for my bride,
Thy image bright still lingers by my side ;
Yes, thou art mine ; thy woman's heart is mine ;
And I am thine ; my heart of hearts is thine.

The Poet's Joy.

Is there a heart to whom the soothing strain
   Of harmony, that wondrous gift divine,
Hath lent not charms soft as the summer rain
   To please the ear melodiously fine?
In joy the bard weaves the immortal line,
   No effort bids him tire his brain with toil;
Free as the wind that shakes the stately pine,
   The flowing muse plays out the ceaseless coil
   That gives the luscious verse, no envy can despoil.

Behold the bard! a meek-faced ruddy youth,
   A blazing eye where kindliness doth rove.
Mark well the glance, the sterling eye of truth,
   That searches deep, deep in the mine of love;
Still unexhausted, still has more to give,
   Seductive task that gently leads the way,
Unearthed the thoughts that evermore shall live;
   Well satisfied, the chords in union play;
   What careth he for fame, what heedeth he for pay?

Give me a day, one hour, in solitude
   Beside the brook where wanton troutlets gleam;
The rocky scaur, half clad with bushy wood,
   Within whose veil ne'er penetrates the beam
Of fiery Sol. 'Tis there, oh! let me dream
   Those golden thoughts that flit across the mind;
All nature to myself, the air doth team
   With things unuttered, noble, pure, refined—
   This is a poet's joy, the sheaves of song to bind.

O, gifted man, to whom the muse is given,
  Would ye refrain from warbling into song ?
Would ye deny the sweetest gift of Heaven
  That ever did to sinful man belong?
Vex not thyself that in the courtly throng
  Thy homely muse doth not her beauties show ;
There is a place for all, for yet among
  The cherished blooms conservatories grow,
    The primrose is as sweet that doth no culture know.

Applause of man, 't is but a passing breath,
  Pleasing the vain ; for flattery is not praise.
Beyond the tomb, beyond the realms of death,
  The hum of fame ne'er penetrates the maze ;
But truth and justice there are shining rays.
  Conscience approved, and all the work well done,
Are anchors sure, and though no mortals gaze
  On the beyond, the great reward is won,
    And life's not been in vain when earth's short
    race is run.

Impetuous stream that plays o'er rock and scaur,
  Foaming the river far below the falls,
Like wild artillery in bloody war,
  Hemmed in on either side by rocky walls ;
The screeching water in its rage recalls
  Stray thoughts of nature in her fiercest style ;
The gallant fish sent backwards headlong sprawls
  On dented boulders, resting there awhile,
    To challenge fate again and leap the watery stile.

Oh ! calm retreat, where innocence doth reign,
   And plenty spreads the board with lavish hand,
What man more joyful than the rustic swain,
   Whose cheerful life with pleasure's arch is spanned ?
Sublime the peace, the solitude is grand—
   Far from the town, the noisy haunt of men,
Unsoiled the air, so little to offend ;
   Blest is his cot in yon green, sheltered fen ;
   He lives a peaceful life in the secluded glen.

At the burnside I pull the violet sweet,
   Wond'ring how so much beauty could be here ;
The gems of earth are squandered round my feet
   In dazzling glory, radiantly fair.
Back on my mind bright memory rushes clear
   To youth's gay days ; again I merry rove
Through woodlands green beside the maid so dear,
   Whose loveliness o'ershadowed all the grove,
   Whose sparkling violet eye was eloquent with love.

Sweet were the dreams we dreamed in yonder glade.
   We carved our names upon the old beech tree,
The song birds paused as holy vows were made
   That made us one for all eternity.
The door of life ope'd on felicity,
   Our happiness was far beyond a name ;
As nectar'd bud invites the honey bee,
   So sweetest love enwrapt us in her flame,
   Consumed the dross of life and purified the same.

Those hallowed scenes still linger on the mind.
   I would not wish that I could them forget ;
Those stores of love so amplified, refined,
   Are nourishment exhaustless—still a debt
Unpaid, unfelt, a light that ne'er shall set,
   A lifelong joy that makes the pathway clear.
A woman's love—no more at fate I fret—
   Has made my manhood virtuous, sincere ;
Love taught me many things, for which I hold it dear.

I love to roam at eve myself alone,
   When curtain'd night excludes the glowing day,
When Venus sits exalted on her throne,
   And brilliant stars their glitt'ring homage pay.
Then wakes the screeching owl to hunt his prey.
   There is a glory in the gloaming hour
That makes me love at eventide to stray,
   Invokes the muse to wield her kingly power,
Strong as the eagle swift, sweet as the opening
    flower.

In solitude the poet finds the muse,
   In solitude he woos the darling maid
That lights his vision with ethereal hues;
   But principally in the greenwood shade
Her royal couch luxuriously is laid
   Beneath the beech upon the gowany sward ;
The favoured ones are there immortal made ;
   Simplicity the luscious verse doth guard,
And Truth, the gem of all, doth crown the tuneful
    bard.

The spring of love he taps with gentle hand,
  Drinks to repletion at the crystal well ;
The burning words await the sweet command
  That makes the passion shine more noble still
Than when in Eden fair it bloom'd at will,
  Or e'er its beauty had been marred by sin.
Like clay in potter's hand he moulds with skill
  The lovely image, pure without, within,
And gains the laurel'd wreath that only few can win.

Perhaps some maid, unconscious of the deed,
  Hath split his heart with those bewitching eyes,
That sparkle like their comrades overhead
  Whose untold glory is in Paradise.
Swift to his harp the raptured poet flies
  And sings of love in strains that never fade,
Enduring as the starry studded skies,
  The picture glows with all the light and shade
That plays a game with time when death him low
      hath laid.

On home-made harp—what though the tone be rude,
  It is his own—he plays with wondrous skill,
He hears the sound and thinks it very good—
  What singer ever thought that he sung ill ?
Bolder he grows, sweeping the strings at will,
  New melody thrills on his raptured ear,
Softer the notes, and circling wider still,
  His touch refined, the harmony comes clear.
He now has found his forte, the minstrel's robes can
      wear.

Creature of impulse, sweeter for the same,
  Thy failings only make thee better loved.
He who would climb the towering heights of fame
  Must first have been by deepest sorrow grieved,
For nature hath to every man bequeathed
  A balancing amount of evil, good.
The mighty painting of the hero wreathed
  Too often hides the dry rot of the wood,
And fame has never brought the happiness it should.

He sees the sun in evening's glory set
  Amid a blaze of tender golden light,
Within his mind the itching dreams beget
  The wish to sing, to paint the landscape bright ;
To him the task is one of pure delight,
  Born for the same, no straining doth annoy
The brain so clear ; selects the language right,
  And weaves the song, the gold without alloy,
A monument of fame, a thing of endless joy.

'T is sweet to be where nature's voice is mute,
  Amid the stillness of th' eternal hills,
Where nothing but the lark's ethereal flute,
  Blent with the hum of the meandering rills,
Attracts the raptured ear, and softly fills
  The ether space.   Pure 's the enjoyment given,
The poet's heart with music wildly thrills ;·
  His inmost soul with ecstacy is riven ;
He leaves dull earth behind to soar far into Heaven.

F

The Kirn.

The sun lay dying in the west
    Upon a couch of yellow ;
A' nature smiled, serenely drest
    In autumn's robes sae mellow.
The last cartload now snugly lay
    Secure up in the barn,
And folk began to tak' their way
    To haud a rantin' kirn,
                  Cheery that nicht.

The herst rig noo o' stooks is cleared,
    The mornin's white an' hoary ;
The simmer heat had disappeared,
    Wi' a' its toil an' glory.
The bonny lads and lasses gay,
    Herts lichtsome as a feather,
Were crackin' jokes alang the way,
    An' trystin' ane anither
                  For reels that nicht.

Braw lasses in the pink o' health
    Love glances shy were hiding ;
The lovely face, unbacked by wealth,
    Wad been a rich providing.
Some trysts which had langsyne begun,
    A crisis now were nearing ;
And others' happiness have won
    Lang ere another shearing—
                  Married that nicht.

Hung roond aboot the kitchen wa's
   Were corn sheaves an' barley;
An' folk cam' troopin' in in raws,
   Some late an' some fu' early.
The table bent 'neath the good things
   That were spread oot in plenty;
An' a' sat doon like queens and kings,
   And every bit as canty
               As them that nicht.

Young Jean the cook, a sonsie queen,
   Fresh as a water lily,
Forgot she had twa restless een,
   That wadna bide off Willie.
While housemaid Kate, a trifle aged,
   Her last engagement ruptured,
Wad fain have had her freedom caged,
   And permanently captured,
               Wi' truith that nicht.

The granary shows a splendid sicht,
   Where violins sweet are sounding;
Where merriment is sparklin' bricht,
   And revelry abounding.
I envy not the foreign chiels
   'Neath sultry skies an' sunny;
My hert is in the Highland reels,
   An' the strathspey sae bonny—
               Alike a' nichts.

My courtly dames, ye dinna ken
   The wealth o' love sae jealous,
That kythes within the bonny glen,
   Far sweeter than the palace.
Gin ye wad see life at the best,
   Sae healthy, happy, hearty;
Gin ye wad ken how puir folk's blest,
   Attend a rural party
               Some orra nicht.

Nae kid-gloved hands were there, I ween,
   For fear ye soiled the dresses;
Nae fashious etiquette between
   The country lads and lasses.
Nae " sirs " nor " mems " had ye to say,
   Wi' speeches highly grammar'd;
'T was juist the hamely " yea " or " nay,"
   In guid Scotch bluntly stammered,
               Wi' them that nicht.

Gi'e royal feasts to learned loons,
   Wi' polite, polished mainners;
Commend me to the plain beef roon's,
   The kail an' tattie denners.
Had oor forefaithers been high fed
   Wi' rich and dainty dishes,
Could Robert Bruce sic heroes led,
   Or made sic glorious dashes,
               Wi' them yon day?

Ae spinster maid, wi' visage sad,
   Sat lang an' ne'er was lifted;
Sair envied her wha had the lad,
   By nature higher gifted;
Till Johnny Pow, the orra hind,
   Went ower an' becked till 'er;
Her wrath subdued, she spak as kind
   As folk when drawin' siller,
              Canty that nicht.

Here clever chiels in skin-meet breeks,
   Braw, bonny lads, an' souple,
Were pittin' in the extra steeks
   Wi' some new-fashioned treeple.
Yet wha wad grudge them honest joys,
   Life's cares for ae nicht casting;
For boys, we ken, will aye be boys,
   And youth 's not everlasting,
              This nor nae nicht.

Oh! wha sae base as wad repent
   He 'd soomed love's sea sae glassy,
Or coont the 'oors unworthy spent,
   Wooin' a bonny lassie?
Those glorious youthfu' days are o'er,
   Gone like a summer morning;
Like waves upon the trackless shore,
   They come without returning
              On ony nicht.

Blythe shepherd Tam an anxious e'e
　　Was on his lassie keepin',
But naething did the laddie see
　　That wad prevent him sleepin'.
Sweet lasses smiled an' joked wi' glee,
　　Sae happy, free, and merry ;
Wi' heids thrawn slightly back agee,
　　Cheeks like the ripest cherry,
　　　　　　　　Rosy that nicht.

Nae wonder laddies' herts did shift
　　Beneath sic rich allurements ;
Yet love's a free an' off-hand gift,
　　That hates a' forced preferments.
But love, true love, can aye be seen
　　Withoot a lang palaver,
And my experience has been
　　That kissin' gangs by favour,
　　　　　　　　Every nicht.

The maister—daicent, canny man—
　　Wi' nae pretence to learnin' ;
A hame-made speech o' welcome span,
　　When twal o'clock was wairnin'.
His e'en grew moist wi' briny dew,
　　He humm'd, he haw'd, he hoastit,
Like Bonaparte at Waterloo,
　　The day he fairly lost it—
　　　　　　　　Upset that nicht.

The nicht wore on wi' sang an' jest—
   Nae time nor tide will tarry—
An' parties broken up are best,
   Ere folk begin to weary.
A reel was ca'd—the hin'maist ane—
   " Miss Lyle," sae sweet an' cheery;
Each laddie took the floor again
   Wi' a selected dearie,
                 Trysted that nicht.

Wi' muckle happy din an' glee,
   They pair off hame returning;
An' 't is a sicht for een to see—
   The break-up in the morning.
Between employer and employed,
   The link has been made closer;
A' ha'in' weel themsels enjoyed,
   And neither side the loser,
                 On ony nicht.

Epistle to Wattie.

Dear Wattie, lad, ye want to ken
How I at first did grip the pen—
   To shy off melancholy—
As ye are ane amang a score,
To you my bosom I 'll lay bare,

Though secrets should be holy;
I 'm no like some wha's rhyme began
  In early youth to dribble;
In years, at least, I was a man,
  Ere I began to scribble.

    Sae happy, the crap aye
      Was ripe for the shearer;
    I lo'ed her, I woo'd her,
      The coortin' aye dearer.

Langsyne, when half way up my teens,
I kenn'd a lass, the queen o' queens;
  She set love's lowe a-flamin';
Her peerless e'e it was the dart
That pierced and kindled in my heart,
  The glorious gift o' rhymin';
So sweet, so dear, so young an' fair,
  Unspeakably bonny,
Nae other lassie could compare—
  A moment wi' my Jenny.

    Though fame should proclaim loud
      My name in floo'ry praise;
    Though sweet be 't, I 'd a' gie 't
      To live again yon days.

Love tapp'd the spring wi' royal pride;
Love opened up the fountain wide;
  Whence gushed the flowing numbers.
Poetic feet unnumbered were,

The harmony was ever there—
    Soft as her rosy slumbers.
Ye ken a' ye wha poets are,
    Ye ken, withoot exception,
The favours that she doth confer
    Are rich beyond description.

      Sae canny, sae bonny,
        She comes na to weary;
      But kissin', caressin',
        The kind little dearie.

My heart was young and soft as wax,
And Love, wha likes sae weel to tax
    The subject she is rulin',
Exacted sair her heavy fee,
An' left me puir as puir could be—
    The price o' her sweet schoolin'.
The love that vexed the saints langsyne,
    An' tarnished sair their glory,
Can still rip hearts like yours an' mine,
    And tear the wound wi' sorrow.

      First love, then, I 'll prove then,
        Is clean away the best;
      A' others it smothers,
        Forgotten when they 're past.

I read your bookie wi' delight;
It minded me o' days sae bright,
    When you the plane was drivin';

Or when yon road ye gaed alang,
The Muse an' you were unco thrang,
    Deep in her pooches divin'.
Imagination is your forte,
  Like Hogg, our Ettrick glory,
But never wi' the fairies sport ;
  Mind wha has been afore 'e.

    Dear Jamie, sae game aye,
      The douce shepherd laddie,
    We maunna, we canna,
      Cross swords wi' oor daddie.

The language that ye like sae weel,
M'Morran gie'd me 't at the schule,
    At Ettrick Bridge End " college ; "
Profound in a' the pairts o' speech,
Nae subject was beyond his reach—
    Far less ootside his knowledge.
Nae doot, like you, I have a place ;
  But where ?   I winna mix it ;
Contented be to run my race,
  Unerring time shall fix it.

    Still singing and stringing
      My pleasures into rhyme,
    Still sliding, confiding,
      Alang the path o' time.

The Feus just now are looking braw;
The turnips fresh, wi' plenty straw—
    A gifty herst time bringin'.
An' then, when a' the crap is in,
The youngsters get a nicht o' fun—
    Sic dancin' an' sic singin'.
Jack Laidlaw's trysted for the ploy—
  And whae can fiddle better?
An' ye'll be there, my canty boy,
  To make the fun the fatter.

    Sic jokin', provokin',
      The rib-rivein laughter,
    Wi' sonnets, off bonnets;
      Twa poets in ae water.

Ye ken I never cared for drink,
In a' my life was never drunk,
    But aye could travel steady;
But gin ye come the Kirn nicht,
I'll no say, lad, but what I micht
    Drink ae wee gless o' toddy.
I mind the first ane I was at,
  Was doon in Fauldshope barn;
Baith in an' oot the nicht was wat—
  It was a glorious Kirn.

    Wi' gettin' an' settin'
      My sweet dear pairtner hame
    'T was morning, adorning,
      Or back the road I came.

I here enclose the princely " Fair,"
When makin 't up I leuch sae sair,
    My face was fair begrutten ;
For graphicness, wild humour gay,
It far surpasses, I may say,
    A' rhyme I 've ever written.
Should ony o' your freen's take ill,
  An' arena like to rally,
Apply the "Fair," the only pill
  Wi' safety they can swallow.

    Sae sure aye, 't will cure aye,
      What other drugs do habble ;
    An' ken 'e, a penny
      Will lift the dwamy trouble.

I 've promised lang to take a turn—
See Ettrick Kirk an' wild Potburn—
    Some bonny simmer morning,
An' view the Napiers' ancient seat,
Embowered among the green woods sweet,
    As hamewards I 'm returning.
Though other vales I yet may see,
  'Neath cloudless skies and sunny,
My heart shall ever be in thee—
  The dearest spot o' ony.

    Sae charmin', sae warmin',
      I spent my boyhood fair,
    An' dyin', still cryin'—
      Let me be buried there.

I now maun gi'e, so here it goes,
My benediction ere I close—
        May joy around you hover ;
Prosperity thy work attend ;
Peace wait thee at the journey's end,
        When this brief life is over !
For why should poets not converse,
   An' freendly be thegither,
Sure, kindred minds are unco scarce ;
   Oft far frae ane anither.

        I 'll hook for, and look for
           A letter frae the bardie ;
        Until then, farewell then,
           Your humble servant, Purdie.

Buccleuch's Rescue of Kinmont Willie.

The night was dark ; the rain in torrents fell ;
And silence reigned in dreary Liddesdale,
Save at one spot where horsemen gathered were,
Equip'd in the habiliments of war.
Two hundred riders, picked from many shires,
Whose blood could claim, untainted from brave sires,
Descent unbroken from an ancient line—
Men famed for deeds that knew not twist nor twine,
Led by the bold Buccleuch—a Border chief,

Whose brave exploits stand out in bold relief
On history's page.   This one eclipsed them all,
And made his fame resound through cot and hall,
Sung by the minstrel bard.   An English lord,
Thought foolishly his country could afford
To treat the lesser sister with disdain.
Valiant Buccleuch made all such projects vain,
And taught mankind a lesson yet unlearned—
That right is right; so he the prison stormed,
And set poor Willie free.   'T was nobly done,
And honour's spurs most gloriously won.
Great noble mind, Scotland hath seldom seen
A braver man.   What other chief, I ween,
Would braved the wrath of England's mighty queen,
Or left her palace victor of the scene?
Haughty Elizabeth, her royal ear
Was unaccustomed to the truth so clear;
Methinks I see her eye a dewdrop woo,
As pale and stern, yet half relenting too,
She heard those words that thrilled her through and
        through—
" Madam, what is there a man dare not do? "
Yes, kings and queens, the pillars of a throne,
Unless supported with more solid stone
Than masonry supplies, unstable are
When discontent becomes a dangerous war.
But empires built on justice, virtue, truth
Shall ever bloom in sweet undying youth,
Where honest worth shall find an honoured place,
And love rule o'er a brave, God-fearing race.

Life.

Oh, sweet wee babe, how calm thou liest now,
The dew of youth upon thy fair young brow,
On thy sweet lips the smiles of childhood play,
As sunbeams dance upon a sunny day.

On thy soft cheek a rosy bloom doth lie,
The tinge of health adds richness to the dye,
While o'er thy face a fragrant light is shed,
Do angels watch and guard thy cradle bed?

Ah, babe, sleep on, thou little reck'st, I ween,
Life is an ever shifting, changing scene;
Full many a flower is smothered in the bud
That promised fair, now numbered with the dead.

Thou knowest not the ups and downs of life,
The smartings 'neath affliction's pruning knife;
Hopes fondly nursed are scattered to the gale,
And idle winds mock at the dreamer's tale.

The cares of life now on thee lightly lie,
And sweet contentment lurks in thy bright eye,
Thy mother's breast, a cure for all thy woes;
Oh, could'st thou there remain, my sweet young rose.

Thou'st yet to learn man's word is not his bond,
That treachery is yawning just beyond,
That grief attends our pilgrimage below;
Earth at the best's a cemetery of woe.

The path of life is aye a thorny way,
Beset with snares to make the pilgrim stray,
At times perplexed what path he should pursue,
Cross roads are thick, the finger posts are new.

What foes, what dangers, we must always brave
In our brief journey to the silent grave,
Head, hand, and heart, are all required to guide
The fragile bark upon the restless tide.

Ah, happy babe, upon thy mother's knee,
There thou dost sit and crow in childish glee;
What shall thy life be?   Ah, but who can tell?
Uncertainty has veiled the future well.

Left in the dark, yet still this much we know,
We have a Friend who lives to plead our woe;
Then trust to Him, His arm is strong to save,
And Heaven illumes the darkness of the grave.

Curlin'.

O' a' the games that e'er I saw,
The game o' curlin' beats them a';
Though ither sports may merry be,
The roarin' game's the game for me.

When a' the hills are cled wi' snaw,
Cauld blaws the wund oot ower the law;
When nose an' cheeks are blue an' blae,
Jock Frost says—"Lads, ye'll sune can play."

Hoo anxiously the ice is tried,
And rash reports are magnified;
Ane gets wat feet; it micht hae borne,
But deil may care, 't will dae the morn.

A ringin' frost the nicht befell,
Next mornin' was as clear's a bell;
The first news was the curlers' hymn—
" The ice is jist in famous trim."

Han'les and stanes are overhauled,
Auld men forget that time has tauld
A tale on them; but cross and wice,
They're off like young chaps to the ice.

The rings are drawn, hog scores are made,
Ilk skip, on whom the duty's laid
To form his rink, sune picks his men;
Noo, heids or tails for the first en'.

" Noo, Johnny, lad, see here's the tee;
A cannie draw jist up to me;
She's weel laid doon; oh, never own 'im;
A fair pat lid; man, Jock, 'e're croon 'im.

The tither skip noo taks his place;
And, wi' a serious, solemn face,
Cries " Tam, this stane is fair tee high
Lay on for here, jist chap an' lie.

G

"Gi'e 'm what ye can—he'll need it a';
Gi'e 'm legs; O Tam, ye 're lookin' braw.
Ye hev 'im deid—hip, hip, hurrah!
Whae was 't that said ye couldna play?

"Noo, Jim, my boy, jist the same play,
But dinna thraw yer stane away.
Gi'e 'm room—stand back; oh, yes, he 'll wing 'im;
If Jock is croon 'im ye are king 'im."

"Losh, Wull, they needna craw sae croose,
There 's no a stane in a' the hoose;
Come, gi'e 's a lead; we 'll let them see
The way to plant them on the tee."

"You for a player!   Man, that's grand;
As shure as daith, as here I stand,
In a' ma life I never saw
A better or a finer draw."

Big Andra fairly felled his stane,
"Han'le 'im—a hog, or I'm mista'en."
Wull stan's an' looks and strokes his baird,
Syne cannily slips on a gaird.

"Ca' up the gaird; I doot ye 've fled 'im;
But never mind; the shot 'll haud him;
Oor side yet for a kittle play.
Shot! besoms up, three cheers, hurrah!

First Love.

Can I forget the love of youth,
Or must I deviate from truth,
To tell about its joys?   Ah, no;
Truth needs no ostentatious show
Her virtues to proclaim.   A lie
At best is but a lie—a stye
Upon the eye of truth.   'T is wise
In man its meanness to despise.
How sweet is love! no word can give
A just idea how first love
Affects the heart of man.   I mind
(As if I could forget) how kind
Its loving tendrils were entwined,
Devoid of cultured, studied art,
Fast, firm around my youthful heart,
There to remain till life's last day,
Until that hour when kindred clay
Lie mingled in the urn.
Bliss never known before made me
Drunk with joy; the world seemed to be
A different one; I lived, but not
As other men lived; my trig boat
Calmly sailed on heavenly seas,
And every breeze was love.   To please
Me creation seemed to have been
Made; my pasture was ever green.
No jaundiced eyes marred my vision,
Love's scales showed no indecision,

No thoughts struggled for division
Within my brain.   Centred on one,
My happy star supremely shone,
The loveliest, the purest stone
Of all the bright galaxy.   Life,
Untroubled with vexation's strife,
Unwounded by the curséd knife
Of jealousy, had pleasures new.
My sky was an unchanging blue,
Adorned with love's delicious hue.
Eye spoke to eye in language plain
I loved and was beloved again.
Blest summit of all earthly bliss,
When pure lips meet in love's first kiss
The whiteness of the stainless snow
Lost its purity 'neath the glow
Of my early love.   Never more
Can my springs of life ever pour
Forth such floods of pure hallowed love
Again.   But once can a heart give
Its all.   I gained a heart (love's shrine),
And gave in all its sweetness mine.
Never more can the dewy kiss
Of woman's mouth be such sweet bliss
To me, or fill with such delight
My raptured soul, as were the sips
I greedy drank from the sweet lips
Of my idol.   No conjecture
Needed, every kiss was nectar.
Yon aged maiden, once so fair

In sunny days of youth, whose hair
Now is streaked with silver, I say go
To her, thou sceptic; she will show
Thee love tokens wealth could not buy.
Perhaps a lock of curly hair
Culled from a lover's brow so fair
Long, long ago. The moistened eye,
Guiltless of palming off a lie,
Loudly tells he is not forgot.
Her heart for him has a green spot.
What matters titles, wealth, or fame,
Are they aye happy who have them?
Remembrance, the costliest gem
That ere adorned love's diadem.

Epistle to Jamie.

While misty fogs besiege the door,
While lads and lasses soondly snore,
I, haein' ae half-hour an' more .
     O' leisure time,
Sit doon, as oft I 've dune before,
     To spin some rhyme.

It 's ill tae ken hoo tae proceed,
Sae muckle rhyme is in my heid,

That must come oot ('t is true indeed),
     Some way or ither.
The bad sae mixed up wi' the guid,
     Jumbled thegither.

My rhyme 's now richt an' workin' rarely,
Tae write it doon, yea, time I 've barely,
It comes sae free, sae fast, an' airly
     Zigzag rowin' ;
Yea, every thing it caps, and fairly
     Cows the gowan.

I dinna mean, far less tae hint,
That I possess what others want ;
In fact my rhyme is juist a rant,
     A metred string ;
But reek, ye ken, maun aye git vent ;
     So I maun sing.

Ae thing I canna understand,
Why gold should be the magic wand,
In sic a bonny fairy land
     As we inhabit,
Why siller does make some sae grand,
     Sae short an' crabbit.

It maitters not, I plainly see,
How otherwise a man may be,
Can he but ready money gi'e,
     To pay his way,
He 's sir'd and honoured, coonted aye
     The time o' day.

Away wi' hollow, false pretence,
Gi'e me the man o' common sense ;
Can either shillings, pounds, or pence
            E'er make a man ?
No, Nature surely had more mense
            Than spoil her plan.

Believe me, things are ordered right,
Though dimly seen by our weak sight,
God, in the wisdom of his might
            And majesty,
Hath made the darkness and the light,
            Gloriously.

God, of a truth, is Nature's God,
Creation doth in every road
Declare his handiworks abroad,
            His praises sing ;
The little daisy on the sod—
            Yea, every thing.

Within my heart, yea, often I
Have wondered how men could deny
That there exists a God on high.
            A drop of dew
Might well convince them that they lie,
            The atheist crew.

How beautiful the fleecy clouds,
The autumn heath, October woods !

They send me off in rhymin' screeds—
    Gudeness kens where
And though I canna ripe the buds,
    My fancy 's there.

Sma' time has only come an' gane
Since I could ca' the muse ma ain ;
But, oh, 't is nice to be ane's lane
    Within her shroud,
And sing her beauties ower again,
    Baith lang an loud.

Of coorse it 's richt eneugh, nae doot,
When ane can bring a volume out,
And to be ca'd a clever cowt
    Is awfu' nice.
Yet some have published, had they not,
    Wad been as wice.

My kind regards to you I send,
My rhymin' billy, trusty friend.
Dear Jamie, lang may love be kenn'd
    'Tween you an me,
And in that world where joys ne'er end
    Together be.

Epistle to Johnny.

I lang hae hed it in ma heid,
Whether for evil or for guid
I dinna ken, tae gi'e a screed
    O' tousy rhyme,
Ca'd poetry.　I daurna dae't
    Juist at this time.

The trees are castin' off their duds
'Neath dull November's leaden cluds,
All silent stand the naked wuds
    In shiverin' line ;
Nae mair we hear the joyous floods
    O' sangs divine.

Hoo sweet the floory month o' May,
When birdies warble on the spray,
The spreadin' hazel, primrose brae,
    In bonny spring,
The lav'rock in the cluds sae hie,
    O' birds the king !

The gapin', glowrin', wanton minnow,
The spreckled parr sae sleek an' canny,
Sport in the bubbling stream fu' funny,
    In harmless glee ;
The eident bee, intent on honey,
    Skims the white lea.

The muircocks browse amang the heather,
Companions o' the whistlin' plover ;
While snug and cosy sleeps the adder
      'Mong breckins green,
Where maukins doze secure a' weather
      'Neath tufted screen.

But hoo 's my sonsie, gifted brother ?
In Hawick there 's nae sic another.
Lang may the Muse, thy bonnie mother,
      Smile sweet on thee ;
And gin she draps anither feather,
      Pray for 't to me.

Thy muse can tak' sublimer flichts,
An' scale Parnassus' lofty hichts,
And revel in their hidden sichts
      Wi' raptured stare,
Than I, or all such prosy wichts,
      Who languish here.

A gross o' thanks for thy kind line.
I hope that a' thy kith and kin
Are in guid health an' thrivin' fine
      Aboot thy bit.
I 'm glad to say that me an' mine
      Are a' afit.

My kindest love I here dae send 'e ;
May a' the poo'rs abune defend 'e,

Watch o'er thy life, an' ever tend 'e
  Frae puirtith's blast ;
May Heaven be, when daith shall end 'e,
  Thy hame at last !

Lasses, Dinna Lee.

Come here, ye bonny lasses a',
  An' rale guid news I 'll gi'e,
For I will tell a tale fu' braw
  Experience tauld to me.

But, lasses, take a bit advice,
  Though gi'en by only me—
Whene'er ye meet a lad that 's nice
  Be cautious hoo ye lee.

The only lad I likit weel
  (I like him to this day)
Cam coortin' like an honest chiel ;
  In jest, I said him nay.

I thocht, as lasses often dae,
  He sune wad come again,
And never to my dying day
  Shall I outlive the pain.

He lo'ed me weel, I brawly knew,
   Love swelled unto the brim;
I lo'ed him in return sae true,
   I wad hae died for him.

But God forgi'e the lee, I pray;
   I suffered for my sin,
And lost into the bargain tae
   The lad I could have won.

Oh, bonny, dainty lasses a',
   Take warnin', dears, frae me;
And whether in a cot or ha'—
   Remember, dinna lee.

To My Wife.

Cheer up your hert, my wee, sweet wife,
   And dinna look sae glum;
Why should the cares o' mairrit life
   Drive frae your cheek the bloom?

The derkest oor, ye ken, sweet dove,
   Is the oor afore the dawn;
And I have pledged my honour, love,
   To be a kind guidman.

Then wherefore should your cheek be pale,
  Your bonnie e'e sae sad?
Hast thou forgot the lover's tale—
  That I am still your lad?

Cheer up, guidwife, and wear the smile,
  Oh, grudge it not to me—
The smile that did me sae beguile
  When you were fancy free.

What though oor backs be tae the wa',
  An' puirtith glow'rin in?
We yet may gowf the gowden ba',
  An' a' oor wishes win.

Though I had a' that wealth could gi'e,
  An' a' that joy could bring,
Unless it were to share 't with thee
  It were a worthless thing.

To Mine Ancient Father in the Muses.

A guid New Year I wish 'e, Mick,
May time be lang ere 'e be sick;
Again, for even countless wealth,
'S nae recompense for want o' health,
Tho' we had millions in oor pooch,
Yet could not leave the sick bed couch;
The meanest vagrant in the fair
Had blessings, lad, we couldna share.

But, man, when we are strong an' weel,
We never think o' being ill;
Sic mournfu' thochts we winna bide,
Health aye as yet 's been on oor side.
But dinna think, robust young man,
Life reaches aye the allotted span;
The strongest trees when rude winds blow
Are aye the first that are laid low.

I wish 'e, Mick, a happy life,
A peacefu' hame unkenn'd tae strife;
May grief aye find a lockit door,
May joys frequent 'e by the score;
Thy wife be a' she oucht tae be,
Sweet mother o' a family;
Like flowers thy smiling babes appear,
Frank, manly, generous, sincere.

Epistle to Willie.

Willie, to warstle time awa,
  I pen you this bit letter;
Though I my spirits won't misca',
  They yiblins hae been better.
But, Willie, I can ne'er forget,
  Till death the link releases,
The hour I met my bonny pet,
  Or how at times she pleases.

Joy of my heart, O darling care,
  To fan the starry flicker
That blazes steady anywhere
  Sae honest, douce, an' siccar.
Alang the fresh green velvet sward,
  Where bonny birds are singin',
On mossy bed reclined the bard,
  His uncouth rhymes is stringin'.

Imagination cleaves the way
  For robes of fancy's knittin',
While music from the hawthorn spray
  Mocks at his tuneless twittin'.
The primrose blinks his dainty e'e
  To catch the early glimmer,
And keps the pearly draps o' dew
  That glorifies the simmer.

The snawdrap peeps its milky crest
  In spring whiles raither hasty,

And sweetly shows 'neath fleecy vest
    Its snaw-white bonnie breastie.
Ah! could I paint bright scenes like these
    With master hand; ah, sketch them
In vain, but aft among the trees
    Delighted oft I watch them.

Dear Willie, send a line or twa,
    Tho' I like ill tae crave ye;
May richer gifts upon you fa'
    Than ever favoured Davie.

Point Medal Day.

'T is medal day; losh, what a steer!
Curlers flock in frae far an' near,
Auld men weel doon life's shady brae
Meet here wi' young chaps blithe an' gay.

Tobacco fabs are toomed a wee,
The fresh-filled mull gangs roond wi' glee,
The couthy flask, wi' cheerin' dram,
Is preed and passed frae Jock to Tam.

Some tak' advantage o' the lull
Tae see gin ice or stanes are dull;
Some work the finger oot, some in,
Some borrow, some lay fair deid on.

The secretary, busy man,
Looks up the " Annual" for the plan,
Tells hoo the rings an' lines should be—
How near an' how far off the tee.

The numbers frae a hat are drawn—
Losh, see hoo yon ane's face is thrawn.
Intae himsel'—" My luck be curst,
Whae ever wan when playin' first ? "

But he leads off as weel 's could be,
The first roond ower, his score stands three ;
The rest a' follow—some mak' ane,
A few unfortunates tak' nane.

The nerves get up on ae auld man,
Doon ower his cheeks big sweat-draps rin ;
At gairds he 's hoggit every stane ;
At drawin', raisin', ne'er made ane.

Doon on their knees some sit an' look,
Thraw oot their airms, bow, gape, and jook,
Rin to the side at ilka stane—
Another blank is scored again.

At strikin', wickin', chap an' lie,
Some steady rin their scores gey high ;
An' true as I 'm a leevin' sinner,
Ane tak's four shots at chip the winner.

H

Ane turns as white as ony sheet,
His looks wad mak a puggy greet,
For merks the buik in vain 's explored,
He 's played a' day an' never scored.

The scores are coonted.   Tam 's eleven ;
His heart 's raised to the seventh heaven ;
Amid loud cries of ": Guid lad, game ! "
Tam proodly tak's the medal hame.

In Memoriam—James Russell, D.D.,
MINISTER OF YARROW.
Died January 9, 1883.

The dear old man has passed away,
   Gone to his rest and glory ;
And now there's nought but dool and wae
   In bonny classic Yarrow.

No more we see his genial face,
   Where beamed with joy each furrow,
Bespeaking kind and courtly grace
   That never had its marrow.

All silent now that matchless tongue,
   Alike in joy or sorrow,
No minstrel's harp more sweetly strung—
   He was thy king, O Yarrow.

His charity it knew no bounds,
  'T was neither scant nor narrow ;
How often hath it gone the rounds
  Among thy dens, O Yarrow?

No more he 'll break the bread of life,
  Nor to his people carry
The message, not of war or strife,
  But peace and love to Yarrow.

The songs that sweet in Zion glide,
  Now dawns a brighter morrow
To him, where crystal streams abide,
  Far purer than the Yarrow.

Safe in the Fold Above.

" Where is my wandering boy to-night ? "
  Safe in the fold above,
Wearing the heavenly robe of white,
  Singing sweet songs of love.

Safe in the blissful land of light,
  Beautiful, fair to see ;
Safe in those glorious mansions bright,
  Safe for eternity.

" Where is my wandering boy to-night ? "
   Where does his head recline ?
On pillows soft, where joys delight,
   Because they are divine—

Where golden harps of sweetest sound
   Give praises unto God,
And all felicities abound
   Within the blest abode.

" Where is my wandering boy to-night ? "
   Sadly the mother sighs ;
Many have perished in the fight,
   And never won the prize.

Bright is the heavenly land so fair,
   Down by the pearly shore.
Mother, your boy shall meet you there,
   Where parting is no more.

Beauty.

Sad ruler of the world. Oh ! fatal gift ;
Worse than poesy, for the poet may
At times sing, to improve the human mind,
Those trying truths felicitously expressed.
Thus Dante wrote. But what good comes from
   thee ?

Thy tendency is but to deform it.
Crippler of the noblest resolutions,
Wise men shun thee; foolish men adore thee.
Cruelly deceptive and seductive
Are the witching smiles of prideful beauty.
The purest of lives have been crushed by thee;
Virtue has been ineffably soiled
By thy sooty hands; and honour dethroned
From its pure and lofty elevation
By the sweet deceivery of thy power.
Have not I myself felt the troublings,
The bitter taunts of an injured conscience—
That executioner acquaint with all—
Pricking like nut-brown thorns that have bedded
In the fleshy couch; and kept not the peace
When, unadvisedly, I left the face,
Plain but honest, for the showy picture,
So soon to be despised? Yet lessons such
As these contain the germ of improvement.
Friendship seared thro' affliction's fire becomes
A thing worth the having. The finest gold
Is lustreless beside a chastened love.
Beauty is nice and fair to look upon—
A silly pride. A noble intellect
'S worth more than a thousand bonnie faces.
Death respects thee not, and cares as little
For thy lily bloom as the vilest weed
That grows unheeded. O, lovely face,
Think not that the spoiler shall not find thee.
The worm, forgetful of thy triumphs here,

Unchecked in the cold grave, shall soon devour
Thy artificial blossom, and feel no
Better fed than when confined to coarser
Victuals.   Such be thy end, sweet face, beware!
Make thy heart as beautiful as thy face;
Then wilt thou become a thing of beauty,
A priceless, undying joy for ever.

Summer Time.

Bright Summer hath come with her gay green bowers,
With her azure skies and her balmy showers.
The ash leaves flutter and bend to the gale,
And joy is abroad in the rural vale.
The lovely flowers, with their beautiful dyes—
The violet, unmatched for its pure, sweet eyes;
The daisies now cover the green fields quite,
The mantle of beauty is spread so bright.

We have waited long, and with patient grace,
For the cheery smiles of thy winsome face;
We have waited long for thy welcome tread,
As the bride adorned for the nuptial bed.
How softly and tender the south winds sigh;
How bonnie the ocean of clear blue sky!
Though the parting is always mixed with pain,
Thou 'rt welcome, aye welcome, to come again.

To John Laidlaw, Hopehouse, Ettrick,

OF VIOLIN RENOWN.

Auld Mother Scotia, honest dame,
  Land of strathspeys an' reels sae bonny,
Among thy sons of violin fame
  John Laidlaw stands as high as ony.

Had Dan M'Pherson, Baillie, Gow
  (Sons worthy of sae kind a mother)
Heard Laidlaw draw his glorious bow,
  Wad claimed him as an elder brother.

The slurrin', quiverin' semitone,
  Wi' him are a' a simple matter;
He aye can be depended on
  To sharp the notes or make them flatter.

How fine his fingers dot the strings!
  To hear him is the highest pleasure;
And what a tone he from them brings!
  The music gets a perfect measure.

Let Austria and Italy brag
  Of Joachim and Paginini;
I 'm thinking, though the preen may jag,
  Nae mony points they could hae gi'en 'e.

Gi'e me Pate Baillie's grand strathspey,
  Wi' Delvinside or Tullogorm,
An' foreign lilts, as weel they may,
  Are smothered in oor Hielant storm.

O, darling Scotia, dearest hame,
　　Land of the rosy, richest splendour,
Protect and guard young Laidlaw's fame,
　　Make his reward of princely grandeur.

Sabbath Bells.

Sweet the Sabbath bells are ringing,
　　Sweet the notes float in the air,
Rousing worshippers, and bringing
　　Them into the house of prayer.

'T is the voice of God that's calling
　　" There is plenty room for all ; "
Let our hearts with joy be swelling,
　　And embrace His gracious call.

Let us, then, our steps be wending,
　　Let us all our voices raise,
Till the angels, condescending,
　　Join our earthly hymn of praise.

Life is fleeting, life is ending ;
　　Let us work while yet 't is day.
Night is coming, fast descending ;
　　Humbly let us watch and pray.

Heaven.

Far from this scene of earthly woe,
  Its sorrows, sins, and tears,
There is a land where pleasures flow,
  And endless spring appears.

There pleasures never know decline
  In all the blest abode;
Where cloudless joys for ever shine
  Around the throne of God.

Disease and suffering 's known no more
  In all the bright domains;
Love blossoms in immortal store,
  And health triumphant reigns.

No eye hath seen that shining land,
  So dazzling, bright, and fair;
No human mind can understand
  What glories shall be there.

There blood-washed souls who here below
  Did love the Lord their King,
And noble martyrs robed in snow,
  Their Maker's praise doth sing.

Can we to all this bliss attain?
  Yes, Christ this gift did give;
Salvation 's free to every man—
  Believe, accept, and live.

Pillars of His Temple.

Pillars of His temple,
  Crowned with glory bright,
Robed in snow-white garments,
  Within the realms of light.

Sweetly are the praises,
  Joyous songs of love;
Happy are the singers,
  Within the courts above.

Where no sin nor sorrow,
  Sickness, pain, or care
Trouble more believers:
  They cannot enter there.

All is love and beauty
  Round the throne on high,
Where the day infinite
  Lighteth all the sky.

Sinners, do not tremble,
  Though pale death doth come;
There 's a mansion ready
  In the heavenly home.

Plunge deep in the fountain,
  Softly He doth call;
Lay your sins on Jesus,
  He can bear them all.

James Thomson,

SHEPHERD, WHITEHOPE, YARROW.
Died Dec. 7, 1882.

The heavens were draped with frozen clouds,
  The snow was fast descending,
The wind drove through the feathery shrouds,
  The drift was almost blinding.
By ten o'clock the storm was fierce,
  And raging most severely;
The snow lay deep; oh! who can pierce
  Out through the wreaths securely?

The shepherd opened wide his door,
  His heart with fear unshaken;
Must my sheep perish on the moor,
  While I have them forsaken?
No! duty calls, I must obey,
  Despite the stormy weather;
Ere time be lost I must away
  My fleecy flocks to gather.

He bravely climbed the mountain's brow,
  The storm aye growing fiercer;
I hear their bleat, I see them now;
  My blood is flowing faster.
The faithful collie round them ran
  The straggling ones to gather;
His master tried to drive them on,
  O! 't was a vain endeavour.

The snow now lay a good yard deep,
   So white and fearful level;
Sunk overpowered, the wearied sheep
   No further could they travel.
By this the landmarks all were lost—
   On his own hill a stranger;
The shepherd felt and knew the cost,
   His own life was in danger.

With staggering limbs and sinking heart,
   The pall of darkness o'er him,
He thought of home, Oh, bitter dart,
   Where joys lay sweet before him.
Sunk 'neath the overwhelming drift,
   A virgin wreath his pillow;
The pale moon in the starry lift,
   Shone like a weeping willow.

The morning sun rose bright and clear,
   The Dowie Dens adorning,
As eager searchers did appear,
   Once more yon Sabbath morning
So near his home the hero lay,
   Embalmed in deathless glory;
And strong men wept their grief away
   In Ettrick and in Yarrow.

Fare-ye-weel, My Bonnie Lass.

Now fare-ye-weel, my bonnie lass,
  May joy an' a' guid things gang wi' thee !
Gin I am spared till Martinmas,
  For auld langsyne I 'll come an' see thee.

O happy, happy we hae been,
  And mony joys we 've had thegither ;
Nought could oor friendship come between,
  Sae unco fond we were o' ither.

Around the kitchen fire at night
  Our taes we toasted on the fender,
While your sweet eyes shed forth a light
  That rested aye on me sae tender.

We built big castles in the air,
  We a' the warld were to each ither ;
We dreamt of future blessings rare
  When some day we'd keep hoose thegither.

We saw sweet bairns around the cot,
  The wee yin toddlin', cryin' " Mammie ; "
May blessings rest on ilka spot
  That boasts o' sic a darling lammie.

But dinna think, though far apart,
  That I can e'er forget my dearie ;
To sing thy praise, my ain sweetheart,
  My tongue and pen shall ne'er grow weary.

John took the Pledge.

John was ill for drink,
　The truth must be told;
And Nancy his wife—
　Her manner was cold.

They courted five years,
　A pretty long while;
But love is so sweet,
　Who counts it a toil?

Then they got married,
　As some people do;
And sometimes I think
　The rash step they rue.

Old slippers were thrown
　For luck, so 't was said;
Unlucky for John,
　For one struck his head.

The honeymoon waned,
　They came back to town
And Nancy displayed
　Her rich wedding gown.

His friends crowded round
　Like bees in a bink;
They all wished him joy,
　While John paid the drink.

His money got scarce,
   His friends they got few;
His credit was gone,
   Which some people knew.

The winter was hard
   Before it was old;
Like Nancy his wife,
   The weather was cold.

John loved not to work—
   A common disease;
'T is nicer by far
   To sit at one's ease.

But John was not born
   To live by his wit,
As some people do,
   And plenty aye get.

So he signed the pledge,
   And touch drink he won't;
What 's more, he 's kept it,
   Which some people don't.

Lord Byron, Poet.

Mighty Byron, the sceptred crown is thine;
Rival thou never hadst.   How tersely sweet
Thy powerful verse, thy eagle muse so fleet;
Winging the heights her glory forth doth shine;
Proud monarch of the art men call divine;
Chieftain of song.   Unparelleled, complete,
Thy rich descriptions are beyond defeat.
The trade mark is embossed on every line.
I love thee, not because thou art a lord,
With all the privileges that birth bestows.;
It was thy gift that drew my heart to thine;
Thy endless wealth of learning I adored.
Safe is thy fame.   Where thy dust doth repose
Shall ever be to poetry the shrine.

In Memoriam.

ARCHIBALD BROWN, ETTRICK SHAWS.

The face I loved so well is gone,
   So honest, free, and fair;   -
The smile where kindness ever shone
   With love beyond compare.

His heart was open as the day;
   Truth was his compass square;
His cheery voice, his Yea or Nay,
   Told manliness was there.

His mind was large, his gifts were great;
    That intellect so keen—
It was my joy, my noble mate,
    Thy comrade to have been.

Communion sweet we often had,
    When others were not near;
My feeble steps were kindly led
    Up to the truth so clear.

Where death, the solemn end of all—
    No life beyond the tomb—
It mattered little when the call
    Conveyed man to his doom.

But far beyond this vale of woe
    There is a land so fair;
Dear Archie, in that land, I know,
    Thy friend shall meet you there.

Oor Wee Darlin'.

Oor wee darlin'—a twalmonth 's gane,
Since oor wee pet frae us was ta'en,
The joy an' licht o' oor fireside,
Her mammie's pet and daidie's pride.

I

Weel dae I mind the joyous hoor
She toddled first across the floor;
She managed fine withoot mishap,
And laid her heid in mammie's lap.

Her wee bit innocent, sweet smile,
Unsoiled wi' sin, unstained wi' guile;
She watched the door when nicht aye came,
Tae gie her daidie welcome hame.

His supper aye wi' her he shared;
Croon'd on his knee, she pu'd his beard;
While mammie sat an' eyed the pair,
Her love divided, balanced fair.

Though oft a tear steals down my cheek,
When at her grave I solace seek,
I know my darlin's noo at rest
Among the babes whom Jesus blest.

'T is hard to pairt wi' those we love,
Yet harder far when a' is taen:
But some day we shall meet above,
And mammie get her pet again.

On the Death of a Poet.

Hail to the shade of our wee bard,
    In peace we did inurn him ;
A quiet spot in yon churchyard,
    Beside the sweet laburnum.

Our cheeks were wet, as well they might,
    Befitting our great sorrow ;
Hope oped her golden gates of light,
    And dawned a bright to-morrow.

The din and noise of life afar
    Ne'er cross the darksome river,
Where love, pure love 's the shining star,
    Whose lustre dimmeth never.

There fields of green, eternal green,
    A lifelong summer morning ;
Perfumed with flowers, a living sheen,
    Adorable, adorning.

A thick veiled cloud of woe and bliss,
    Unpierced by living mortal,
Is hung between that land and this ;
    Faith is the only portal

Whence we can join the sacred throng.
    Sin is our great deceiver;
Till overcome we hymn our song,
    The joys of a believer.

Lines Addressed to a Violin.

Sweetest instrument I know,
Magic music 's in the bow ;
Beautiful thy tone, so clear,
Ravishing both heart and ear.
Glorious thy harmony,
Queen of sweetest melody ;
In the homes of poor and great
Thou art found enthroned in state.
Prince and peasant homage pay
To thy sweet, unrivalled sway.
On the happy bridal morn,
At the roaring country kirn,
Thou art ne'er unwelcome guest,
Purest instrument and best.
O how vain to sing thy praise—
Polkas, Highland reels, strathspeys,
Are interpreted by thee
In the choicest melody.
Charming sweet 's the " Brig o' Dee,"
Or Pate Baillie's grand strathspey ;
But to hear thee in thy pride
Thou must give me " Delvinside."
But it needs not song of mine
To make all thy beauties shine.
He who first thee did invent
Unto all the world hath lent
Evidence of genius bright,
·Grander than the poet's might.

He whose fingers first caress'd
Lovingly thy matchless breast,
Sweet and peaceful be his rest!
Glorious thy harmony,
Queen of sweetest melody!

What My Love is Like.

I 'll tell you what my love is like,
   The lass that I lo'e best o' a';
Her form is of an angel make,
   Her bosom 's purer than the snaw.

I 've seen the sun in simmer set
   Far i' the west 'mid golden rays;
I 've seen the rosebud dewy wet,
   Sae bonnie far ayont a' praise.

I 've seen the woodlands in their pride
   Wi' flowers o' every kind and hue;
But Nature, love, has lavished wide
   Her choicest sweets to garland you.

Sweet Isabel, my darling love,
   Sweet empress of my heart and soul,
Without thee life would misery prove;
   With thee how sweet, though thou wert all.

Thoughts on the Old Year.

Another year is on the wing,
   But have we spent it well?
To what side doth the balance swing?
   Alone let conscience tell.

Have we been true unto ourselves,
   Employed the talent given,
Or has 't lain rusting on the shelves,
   No interest in Heaven.

Have we assisted with our wealth
   The helpless and forlorn?
Have we been thankful for the health—
   The rose without the thorn—

That was vouchsafed to us each day,
   In purest, richest store?
Dear friends have swiftly passed away,
   And now are known no more.

Have we amid those precious hours
   Planted the seed of faith,
That shall adorn with rosy flowers
   The solemn bed of death?

Nae Game like Curlin'.

The grund was hard, the frost was keen,
The glitterin' ice lay like a sheen
O' silver white, while Crawfordjohns,
Nice Burnocks, Ailsa Craigs, and Hons
    Were put in trim for curlin'.

The clachan 's fair deserted—clean ;
Aboot the place nae men are seen,
But bairns are yellin' at their play—
" We winna get oor licks the day,
    The Maister 's at the curlin'."

The parish priest, wi' reverent face,
Can tak' and gi'e a joke wi' grace,
Enjoy himsel' like ither men—
There 's nae distinctions here, ye ken ;
    We 're brithers a' when curlin'.

The game proceeds ; the fun is guid—
Nae danger here o' frozen bluid ;
Adoon oor cheeks the sweat-draps rin,
Like splashin' spray oot ower a linn,
    At the roarin' game o' curlin'.

" Losh, soop her up ! man, bring 'er on ;
She 'll get a chip and gaird the stone ;
Stop noo—haud up !—the vera thing.
Man, Jock, ye 're juist a curlin' king."
    There 's nae game like curlin'.

"Ye see that pat-lid on the tee?
Man, Tam, play that yin oot for me;
Ye've dune't afore—clear oot the lot!
She's portin' grand—Hoo! shot! shot! shot!"
          There's nae game like curlin'.

"Man, for a gaird; oh, noo, be shuir;
Plant weel yer feet; be cautious there:
Haud off the broom! be cannie noo—
Ye've played it, lad!—Huroo! Huroo!"
          There's nae game like curlin'.

"Jim, tak' an inwick off this stane,
And sune we'll lie the shot again;
They little ken yer skeel, I wot;
Ye lick a' for a kittle shot
          At the slid game o' curlin'."

"Noo, Bauldy, ye've the hin'mist stane;
They're three aheed—that fact is plain;
Tak' this yin oot, and we lie four.
Ye've dune it weel—we tap the score!"
          There's nae game like curlin'.

Lines on George Lord Byron.

It needs no bronze nor marble bust to keep alive his
    name,
Each wave upon the ocean's breast but adds to
    Byron's fame;
And Time's destroying chisel strong may hew at it
    in vain;
Hid, like the sun behind a cloud, to shine more
    bright again.

Enshrined within a nation's heart, his name shall
    never die;
Magnificent's yon comet star, the glory of the sky;
The other stars that round him shine all sweet
    allegiance own,
Unchallenged in his royal right to wear the
    monarch's crown.

Enthroned upon his princely couch, the sweetest bed
    of song,
By what magnetic influence draws he the listening
    throng?
'T is that of song, and sweet the sound that flows
    serenely on;
A master's touch alone can bring so ravishing a
    tone.

And Byron's was a master's hand, we feel it as he
      sings ;
The eloquence of all the chords, the trembling of the
      strings,
The passions of the human heart, its depth, its
      breadth, its length,
Are interwoven in the chain of matchless beauty,
      strength.

Crowned on the lofty hill of rhyme, methinks I see
      him now,
His calm and clear majestic eye, his intellectual
      brow ;
Oh, for a pen like his, that I may wield it at my will,
To picture England's greatest bard with all the
      artist's skill.

But, ah ! it needs not pen like mine, nor lisping
      tuneless song
To sing his praise, the wind that blows doth carry it
      along ;
The fragrance of the budding rose burns incense to
      his fame,
And long as poetry is read shall live Lord Byron's
      name.

Ae Simmer Nicht.

Twa couples braw ae simmer nicht
   On Shaws hill did forgether,
Tae view the glowing landscape bricht,
   And scent the fragrant heather.
Deep in their hearts love had its seat,
   That shrine of sweet devotion,
That shrine that makes a barren state
   Smile like the land of Goshen.

Twa nicer lasses ne'er were seen,
   Were ne'er eclipsed by ony;
I muckle doot if Burns's Jean
   Looked half sae sweet or bonny.
The lads looked pleased, as weel they micht,
   Their glances were most tender;
The lasses were uncommon bricht,
   And couldna hae been kinder.

Oh ! love, pure love, nought can excel
   Thy influence majestic;
The hardest heart beneath thy spell
   Becomes soft and elastic.
The lovely scenery was grand,
   An' glorious athegither;
Wild violets bloomed on ilka hand
   Among the bloomin' heather.

The larks sang sweetly up abune,
  Their splendid music trilling,
While doon below that efternune
  Responsive echoes, willing,
Went up and joined the choir above
  In blissful exultation,
And every chord was chanting love
  In joyous adoration.

The courtier may smoother speak
  Wi' words refined and ready,
And volley cannonades o' reek,
  Prefaced aye wi' " My lady."
Oh, could he leave the gay saloon,
  Wi' a' its pomp an' glitter,
To revel wild this afternoon,
  And taste the sweets o' Natur.

Oh, wad he leave the princely show
  O' money, pride, an' fashion,
For yon sweet glen where, far below,
  Yon bonnie lassie 's washin'.
She spreads her claes upon the green,
  And laves the burnie ower them,
An' meets her lad at dewy e'en
  Where naebody can glower them.

In bidding them a sweet good-bye,
  May Fate aye prove propitious,

To shower upon them every joy
    That can make life delicious.
May strength, an' health, an' plenty wealth
    Be aye within their hallan ;
May poverty an' ill-health be
    Aye strangers at their dwellin'.

Yarrow.

Have mercy on my aching brain,
    My keen conception spare O—
Who ever thought I 'd hear again
    That sung-to-death stream, Yarrow !

Sma' wonder that my thochts gang wrang,
    My muse chirps like a sparrow,
Gang where ye like, the same auld sang
    Is Yarrow, ever Yarrow.

Has Scotland only ae spot green,
    Its boundaries sae narrow,
That tourists ne'er the world have seen,
    Unless they 'd been in Yarrow.

I 've been ower a' the " Dowie Dens,"
    In rain and sunny weather,
But never saw the bonnie glens—
    Just common hills and heather.

It micht be that my sicht was biassed,
　　So missed the fine reflection ;
If not, thy sweets were a' disguised
　　From one poor bard's detection.

Another book, enough of this—
　　Yarrow's threadbare already ;
Of course where ignorance is bliss,
　　Wisdom's a foolish lady.

I doot some winna be weel pleased
　　At my weel-meant oration ;
But let them be—far better teased
　　Than killed wi' adulation.

Ettrick, cock up, haud up thy heid,
　　Thou hast no cause for sorrow ;
A share of gifts are o'er thee spread,
　　As rich as bloom in Yarrow.

Big Drucken Wull.

This story that I 'm gaun to tell
　　Is neither unco strange nor queer,
It 's a' aboot big Drucken Wull,
　　That signed the pledge juist last New Year.
Wull was a joiner to his trade,
　　A clever, handy man was he ;
But every nicht his wage was paid
　　That nicht he aye got on the spree.

He wasna fear'd to stand a round,
　　Be 't either sweet or bitter ale ;
A blyther lad could not be found
　　Than Wull when he was 'bout half sail.
The sangs he sang were aye the best,
　　Sangs o' the guid auld Burns kind ;
There 's noucht like them to stand the test—
　　Sangs nooadays are sae refined.

Forbye he played the fiddle too,
　　A better never wielded bow
Since Scotia lost long, long ago
　　The famous gifted chiel ca'd Gow.
Syne when aff hame he set at last,
　　He scarcely could vacate his chair ;
Wi' swaggering gait, unsteady step,
　　He 'd whiles sair play to find the door.

Not that he didna ken the place,
　　But then his eyes saw things so queer,
And magnified at sic a pace ;
　　Nae wonder oft he wasna sure.
His bonnie Jeanie oft was vexed
　　To see her man to drink a slave ;
Her temper oft was sorely taxed,
　　And sadly oft her heart misgave.

Experiments were tried in vain
　　To wean him from the public-hoose.
But such the stubbornness of men,
　　As weel hae spoken tae a mouse.

But accidents hae aye a cause,
   When we the weak point can discern ;
And nae man yet sae clever was
   But aye saw something he could learn.

Atweel, to make my story short,
   As I believe some's whiles ower lang,
Wull was a chap of the richt sort,
   'T was a' the drink that put him wrang.
Ae nicht he set off to a ball,
   And drink ye may be shure was there;
And lang before the hour o' twal
   I'm certain Wull had ta'en his share.

He set off hame in merry mood,
   Ne'er dreaming what would him befall ;
Or that again he never would
   Drink, handle, touch, or taste at all.
A quarry hole lay in his way,
   But then his e'en were dazed wi' drink
Or he Jock Robison could say,
   His leg was broken in a wink.

The miseries he did endure,
   Till he was rescued later on,
Had pairt ado, you may be sure,
   When he our Band of Hope did join.
Frae that nicht even to this time
   A steadier man there couldna be ;
Peace and contentment reign at hame
   And love blinks sweet in Jeanie's e'e.

Sonnet—Scotland.

Dear Auld Scotland, the dearest land on earth,
My blood dances with joy to hear thee praised.
Other lands may boast of a purer sun,
Where the sky is ever clear, where the fig
Tree and the rich orange tree blossom in
Unequalled splendour, where one has only
To stretch forth and pluck luxurious fruits.
But what are these to me? Thou hast a charm
For me, for art thou not the land of my
Nativity? I drew on thy hallowed
Soil my first breath of life, and on it I
Will draw my last. Thy heather-clad mountains,
With their towering peaks, where the eagle hath
His eerie, where the lark soars till he is
Lost in the fleecy clouds, where the foxglove
Nods in majestic stateliness to me,
Are dearer far than all the lands on earth.
The cradle of liberty was rocked in
Thy solitary glens. Here freedom's muse
Lisped its sweet numbers and rolled into a
Wealth of song, that made thee the queen of
Nations and exalted thy fame to heaven.
Thy noble son, the heroic Wallace,
Unfurled his banners and bade defiance
To thy Southern foes, that thou mightest be free.
Foully betrayed, inhumanly butchered,
His spirit still haunts his native valleys,
And Scotland exults o'er her darling son.

K

'T was on the green haughs of Caledonia
That lovely Coila, with modest mein, threw
Her mantle o'er Robert Burns, and tuned his
Harp to sing those artless notes that hath charmed
The ears of a world.   The crown of berries
That she placed on his manly brow, instead
Of losing their brightness, to-day are as
Rosy as that hour she crowned him ; and where-
Ever poetry is read and genius
Adored thy national bard occupies   '
An honoured niche in the temple of fame.
Oh, dear Scotia, my beloved country,
Thy mists are more congenial to me
Than the sunshine of France or Italy.
Where shall I find brave sons like Scotland's sons ?
Where, oh where, shall I find bonny lasses
That for beauty can take the pass off thine ?
The rosy cheek and the soft, sparkling eye,
Where love luxuriates, proclaims the fact
That beauty thrives in thy northern home,
And is perfected in thy misty clime.
Oh, darling Scotland, what more can I say
Of thee, most favoured nation under Heaven ?
Thou hast a goodly heritage; may peace
Abound within thy walls, and joy, love, and
Prosperity within thy palaces !

Sonnet—Death.

Death comes to all men whether they try to
Avoid it or not.   None are exempted ;
The millionaire on his princely bed, as
Well as the beggar on his lowly cot,
Must pass through those portals, from whence there
    is
No returning.   Of what use are millions
To him now ?   He must die and leave them all ;
Yea, die as poor as he had had them not.
Oh that men would live so as they could die !
The Christian can meet thee with unblanched
Countenance, and tell thee bluntly to thy
Face thou hast no terrors for him ; he can
Even welcome thee to his bosom as
His dearest friend and kindest physician.
Thy medicine to the sinner may be
A little too purging, yet to him it
Is the queen of drugs, the passport to heaven.
O Death, thou art only but the ladder
By which we mount to the regions of bliss,
Where the fountains of joy are opened, where
The souls of just men shall revel in all
The innocent pleasures of the redeemed.
It is a very solemn thing to die ;
But, my friends, it is much more so to live ;
Dost thou want to see a man in his true
Colours ?   Yes, you do.   Well, then, come with me.

You see yon sick bed, and its occupant?
He is dying, and he knows it.   Ask him
If he is prepared to speak the truth.   The
Look he gives you will be answer enough.
Art thou satisfied?   Need'st thou other proof?
This is the truest moment of his life.
Death, thou hast no victory to boast of;
Why should we fear thee?   Trust in God, and we
Are safe; safe for time and eternity.

Sonnet—Peace.

Peace, how glorious are all thy blessings!
In thy rest the wearied soul finds repose,
And saith to itself, yea verily I
Will make my habitation here: here is
My rest and stay, for I do love it well.
Thou art no mischief-maker, thou hast no
Delight in brawls; from thy beautiful lips
The words of love in purity do flow.
Thou art no respecter of persons, thou
Dwellest as frankly 'neath the thatched roof
As in the corniced halls of royalty.
The monarch on whose brow the diamonds blaze,
To whose slightest nod men bow obedience,

May yet be a total stranger to thee,
And never know the worth of happiness ;
While a humble casket may conceal the
Jewel that can neither be bought nor sold.
How rich the altar of thy sanctuary,
From whence smokes the clouded incense of love.
Thou makest life enjoyable ; to the soul
Who finds thee paradise has been regained,
And, best of all, no more again be lost.
The soldier, inured to the din of war
And the strife of camps, longs for the time when
The bugles shall sound the notes of peace, and
The scarlet lines shall melt to form no more ;
When the cruel sword, varnished with human
Blood, shall no more decide disputes, but leave
The issues with his more powerful brother—
That noble instrument men call the pen.
Oh, that men would give up the strife of war,
And glory in the nobler paths of peace.

The Hazel Glen.

Dearly I love the hazel glen,
　In the summer bright and sunny ;
The lark sings sweet above my head,
　And the primrose bank is bonny.

The pure air clears the wearied brain,
　Prepares the mind for thinking ;
Down on the grass I musing lie,
　The chain of life new linking.

I hear the river sounding on—
　O'er rocky throat it gurgles ;
Far down below, around the foam,
　The waltzing bubble sparkles.

The gleg-eyed weasel hunts his prey,
　By fairy rings undaunted,
Where fairies langsyne held the dance,
　And simple folk enchanted.

Here sweetest flowers of richest hues
　Grow where the green leaves shade them ;
Beneath yon stone, true martyrs lie,
　Where persecution laid them.

Give studied art to those who wish,
　Give wealth to fools to squander ;
Give me the glory of the glen,
　With freedom there to wander.

The Turkish Atrocities.

Brave Albion, put forth thy might,
  Proud mistress of the sea—
Bold champion of every right,
  And glorious liberty.

To whom could weak Armenia cry,
  But to the people brave?
The land where Bruce and Cromwell lie,
  Where jaggy thistles wave.

O Britain, by thy glorious fame,
  That makes the tyrant fear ;
By all humanity can name,
  Or liberty hold dear,

Go forth and stop the brutal work.
  To stay thy hand none dare ;
And, if need be, remove the Turk
  From off God's landscape fair.

Ten thousand of our kilted lads
  Could marches redd, I ween ;
Sweet maids would bless the tartan plaids
  That made their sleep serene.

The horrors done on Turkish soil,
  Where crime and lust prevail—
It makes the British blood to boil,
  To read the shameful tale.

The False Lover.

With heavy heart I pen this note in answer to thine
    own ;
How sad to think that thou art false ; oh, had I only
    known !
But now I write to let thee know that thou art once
    more free ;
Thy secret I will closely guard, that once thou
    lovedst me.

Oh, where are all thy solemn vows and honied words
    so sweet ?
A maiden's love thou hast betrayed, and trampled
    'neath thy feet ;
But still the love I bear to you my tongue can never
    tell ;
My love to hatred ne'er could turn ; for I have loved
    too well.

'T is sad to think that all my love should thus be
    thrown away ;
A broken heart is my reward, my rest a bed of clay ;
And when my grave is withered bare—the snow lies
    on the braes—
My spirit, in the spirit land, shall wish you well
    always.

For if the God who rules above can e'er forgive your
    sin,
It to your charge shall ne'er be laid by your forsaken
    one ;
Though thou a traitor proved to me, and robbed me
    of my joy,
My bleeding heart to you doth wish a sweet, a sweet
    good-bye.

Sunset.

The setting sun glorious shone
'Mid a sea of blue; far upon
The vaulted space the parting rays
Set all the sky into a blaze
Of blended light; the dark recess
Of green shaggy wood made no less
Sweet the scene.   Piping on each bush,
Feather'd songsters encored the thrush
With lusty vigour; such a scene
Is beautiful, before the green
Summer merges into the brown
Of mellow autumn's golden crown—
Exquisite, magnificent, grand,
Sweet as a dream of fairyland.

Rural Poetry.

Untutored in poetic art,
Unknown at her auction mart,
Fit subject for vile critic sport,
      While smaller fry,
Like echoes distant rocks impart,
      Tak' up the cry.

The rustic bard is hunted doon,
Puir silly, crack'd, demented clown,
That scarcely kens a harvest moon
      Frae 'mong the others ;
Forsaken, friendless, left tae droon
      'Mong lots o' haivers.

Hail poesy ! thou queen enthroned,
How often hath thy life been maimed,
Or thy majestic shin banes lamed
      By prosy fetters,
And thy sublimity inflamed
      Wi' dull Greek letters.

While thy true sons by thee inspired,
The glowing eye by genius fired,
The language all that is desired,
      The guid braid tongue ;
How sweet the sang, like lightning wired,
      Thy bards have sung.

O bonnie hill o' sweet Parnass',
How mony a Greek an' Latin ass
Hath fondly wooed thee for his lass,
   But all in vain;
Half fell'd, disjaskit, on the grass,
    For weeks he's lain.

Just as I write this sonnet queer,
A bonnie bird is whistling near,
Its melody, sae sweet and clear,
   Thrills through my heart;
Each note says, take a lesson here
    From nature's art.

Among the bonnie brackens green,
The wavin' corn at dewy een,
The trottin' burnie's misty sheen,
   The jappin' spray,
Contentedly, by a' unseen,
    I rhyme away.

'Mong sweet blue bells the mountain air
Blaws fresh and caller everywhere,
Eneugh and plenty aye to spare
   To smoky toons,
Where wives an' sickly weans pine sair,
    Wi' heidache croons.

How nice the fields at even tide,
When nature looks braw as a bride,

Disgorgin' flowers in heidlang flood
        Across the earth,
While spring, the howdy wife, wi' pride
        Assists at birth.

Or winter wi' his hoary pow,
The meltin' wreaths, the roarin' thow,
The rattlin' ice boards wildly row
        Frae side to side,
And flooding ilka haugh an' howe,
      . Deep, fer and wide.

The Lovers Reconciled.

With joyous, lightsome heart I write to let my
    darling know
He's lifted from my wearied breast a heavy load of
    woe ;
Thrice happy was I to receive your kind and
    welcome line ;
Blest consolation 'tis to know your heart beats true
    to mine.

But wherefore did you send me word that you had
    changed your mind ?
Which of the two must I believe that I the truth
    may find ?

I must confess I am perplexed between those **letters**
    two ;
The first one showed that you were false, the second
    proved you true.

But since you say that you are true, and still **my** ·
    · own dear lad,
To test the truth of what you say I purpose **to get**
    wed ;
Put in the banns, make no delay, and see that **all is**
    square ;
And happy, happy is that home when love's **a**
    dweller there.

No more to part, but always love, how happy **we**
    shall be ;
Tho' poor our lot, our cot will be a paradise to me,
Where we shall taste the sweetest joys that ever
    mortals knew,
And live a sweet, contented life—devoted, faithful,
    true.

Only Six Years.

Only six years, my darling boy,
    Thy life was scarce begun
Ere thou wert called to taste Heaven's joy,
    And wear its golden crown.

Only six years ! to me it seems
  Thy life was but a day,
And thy fond mother's hopeful dreams
  Of manhood, where are they ?

Only six years, my little flower;
  Since thou to earth did come ;
But now eternal in that bower,
  Thy Heavenly Father's home.
Only six years ! We meet again,
  Yes, meet to part no more ;
Complete in Heaven 's the broken chain—
  Thou art but gone before.

To my Isabel.

Dear Isabella, sweetest maid
That ere the heart of man did move,
Sweet as the rosebud tint arrayed,
Bright as yon twinkling orbs above,
Pure as the snowdrop in the glade,
Or sweetest violet in the grove,
Or lovely moss rose in the shade,
All want the sweetness of my love.

Dear to my soul and inmost heart,
Life were a blank without thy smile;
How fond to meet, how sad to part,
Though only for a little while;
Oh how devoid is love of art,
A stranger to dishonoured guile,
How sensitive to every smart,
Or ecstasy that thrills the soul.

Accept this pledge of love, sweet maid,
Which this poor card to you conveys;
May every mountain, stream, and flood,
The rocky glens, the daisied braes,
Combined with virtue's powerful aid,
The swelling chorus joyful raise,
Till universal nature wide,
Proclaim aloud my darling's praise.

Oh, Thou the Great All-seeing Power,
Oh, hear my ardent, fervent prayer,
Watch o'er and tend my darling flower,
Make her Thy most peculiar care!
Oh, guard her footsteps every hour
From foul temptation's fatal snare,
And lead her to that blissful bower,
Where joys eternal blossom fair.

Ettrick.

Oh ! river of my boyhood's mirth,
  Oh ! river of my native dale,
To me the dearest spot on earth
  Is Ettrick's quiet, peaceful vale.

When spring, the charming damsel, green,
  Wi' snawdraps cleads thy bonnie braes,
The primrose bank so sweet, serene,
  Were a' beyond my power to praise.

When autumn wi' its yellow crest
  Brown'd deep my bonnie Forest grey,
Thou bonnie stream, that I lo'e best,
  Wi' joy I've heard thy ripplets play.

When winter rains did fiercely blaw
  And tinged thy placid waters clear,
I've listened to thy roaring fa'—
  The music I so loved to hear.

And now that I am leaving thee,
  The parting—oh, it gives me pain ;
Though grim despair looms gloomily,
  Hope whispers, " We may meet again."

Fareweel, my comrades, ane an' a',
  The playmates of my early years—
The joys we've had are a' awa',
  Like snaw-wreaths when the thow appears.

Jottings.

She trusted me.   Her love was ocean deep,
  Boundless as air, pure as the blue above,
Strong as the bolts that priceless jewels keep;
  O, what a precious thing is woman's love!
We both were young—life then is sweet to live—
  We never saw the fields so green before,
Nor knew that life such happiness could give:
    Two souls, yet one in union evermore,
    Locked in each other's arms the rain of love did pour.

Our tongues were mute, we communed with our eyes,
  In language richer far than pen could write;
Their liquid softness shamed the balmy skies,
  Their brilliancy eclipsed the stars at night.
Love was our sun, we saw no other light;
  It was enough, we loved as few have done;
But destiny, that worketh ever right,
    Diverged our paths; cross purposes were run;
    Stern fate closed up the book auspiciously begun.

Sweet is the glen where beauty sleeps unseen,
  The stately foxglove rears its head on high;
With hazelly banks the burnie runs between,
  Fed by the spring no sultry sun can dry;
So fresh the green, so soothing to the eye
  Jaded with toil; the weary brow of care
Can here relax, anxiety defy.
    O lovely glen! thy jewelled sward so rare
    Would make an ideal grave, so calm and peaceful
      there.

L

Vain is the man who for ambition toils,
  Destroying health for such a bauble vain ;
Deceitful glory, what are all thy spoils ?
  Too oft regretted by a life-long pain ;
Oh, give me virtue's path, unrugged, plain —
  The mind serene, contentment's sweetest bliss ;
Then in yon hour life has not been in vain.
  What pleasure is 't the cup of joy to kiss,
  If we the great reward, the crown of life, do miss ?

'T was thee, sweet maid, that woke my muse to sing,
  Nor think it strange that I should sing of thee ;
To sing of thee doth ever pleasure bring ;
  I nurse the thought because it pleases me.
My fancy roams oft to the trysting tree,
  Sacred because thy name is on the stem.
Ah ! happy youth, the hours right pleasantly
  Were freely spent, unknown those dreams of fame,
  That tease the after life in fortune's fickle game.

Give me the brook, the cool and shady grove,
  Where nature's sweets at random are displayed ;
There I can read deep in the book of love,
  Again caress and converse with the maid
Who, to my eye, by fancy's kindly aid,
  Is ever young.   I see again those eyes—
Two starry dewdrops, with a purer shade
  Than ever blazed at eve in diamond skies—
  I commune with her yet, for true love never dies.

O, who can gauge the depth of woman's love?
   What mind can grasp the sweetness of the same?
Its constancy no logic can disprove,
   No envy blur the whiteness of the flame,
Nor death destroy the fragrance of its name.
   Its worth to me my tongue can never tell,
Alike in hours of poverty and fame,
   Sweet as the moss rose in the shady dell ;
Oft have I sung of love, the theme I love so well.

O, wearied heart, that found at last its mate,
   Green were thy joys in youth's gay, sunny days.
Could ever wealth or friendship of the great
   Bestow on life these juicy, palmy rays
That melt the heart when in the rosy maze
   Of love's gay dance we waltzed dull care away ?
Too good to hate, too beautiful to praise,
   Life was compressed into a summer day,
   Where flowers for ever bloomed in lovely land-
      scapes gay.

With arm in arm we strolled beneath the shade
   Of leafy trees, in Brockhill's flowery grove ;
Sweet were the tunes the band above us played—
   Enchanting airs so redolent of love.
Love, glorious love ! meek as a turtle dove,
   Attended us with all her gifts divine ;
We were on earth, but far in heaven above
   Our minds did roam, where pleasures ne'er decline ;
   Our thoughts were poetry deliciously fine.

Behold the sun in majesty arise
   From ocean'd pillows bathed in deepest blue ;
Sweeping across the vast unmeasured skies,
   His daily routine journey doth pursue.
Rising at eve, when falls the gentle dew
   O'er palmy isles, shedding his rays serene ;
Spreading a glory Scotland never knew—
   Where through the year the leaf is ever green ;
   Where east winds are unknown, and snowflakes
      never seen.

But dearer far are Scotia's mountains wild,
   Where screaming eagles freedom do proclaim,
And rocky glens where liberty beheld
   With streaming eyes heroic deeds of fame.
Wallace and Bruce, with others I could name,
   Whose claymores swept the tyrant to his grave,
The tartan plaids aye set my heart on flame,
   And heather red, where stalwart thistles wave,
   Guarding our bonnie fatherland Scotland the
      brave.

O, Scotia, dear ! Land of the Heaven-taught bard,
   Of foaming floods, and towering mountains green,
Around thy shores the rolling waves keep guard :
   Within thy homes are gallant hearts, I ween.
Safe is the throne of our belovéd Queen—
   Complacently we gaze across the sea
Upon the world ; our slumbers are serene ;
   The bagpipes sound the notes of liberty,
   For Scotsmen aye have been and ever shall be free.

Oh, come my muse, and strike a major key!
   The pith is thine, the instrument is tuned,
And sing a song of sweetest melody,
   That to thy fame and credit shall redound,
When daisies white bloom o'er the singer's mound,
   And pilgrims come to gaze with wond'ring eyes
Upon the harp that gave so sweet a sound;
   Know thine own power, on eagle's wings arise,
   Earth never was thy home, thou lived in purer skies.

For I have sung so oft of love that I
   Am half afraid my song is growing stale,
Yet 't is a subject wide as earth and sky,
   And ever shall remain the sweetest tale.
But, hark! my muse, I hear the cuckoo's wail;
   'T is spring again, the woods are waving green,
And softer winds invade the flowery dale,
   Where truant snows did loiter long, I ween—
   How changed the landscape now; O, what a
     lovely scene!

Jeanie's Bonnie, Jeanie's Sweet.

Her rosy cheeks aglow wi' health
   Would ornament a palace ha';
But dearer far than untold wealth,
   Because she lo'es me best o' a'.

     CHORUS.—Jeanie's bonnie, Jeanie's sweet,
        And she has twa sic bonnie een;
      Jeanie's modest, trig, an' neat,
        The sweetest flower I 've ever seen.

Her smile would make the slave forget
  The precious want of liberty.
I 'll ne'er forget the hour we met
  When Jeanie pledged her love to me.

The mavis sang his sweetest sang
  As gloamin' did her curtains draw ;
Wi' love we thocht the time nae lang,
  For it will aye be king o' a'.

Wi' ae fond kiss and sweet embrace—
  Kind love it was between us twa ;
Nae jealous thochts my mind did chase,
  For Jeanie lo'es me best o' a'.

Jenny, Love.

Oh, Jenny, love! sweet Jenny, love,
  Sair is the breast forsaken ;
Some pity have an' let me live,
  My wearied heart is breakin'.

My youthfu' heart ye stole awa
  The first time I was near 'e ;
Gi'e me yer ain, ye need na twa,
  My sweet an' bonnie dearie.

O, wha can look into thine eyes
  But ever after bless them ;
Or near those lips an' not arise
  The burning wish to kiss them ?

The blushing rose, wi' tender grace,
  Doth yield the palm serenely,
Forgets her ain sweet royal face
  To gaze on one more queenly.

Isabel.

Let poets sing, their voices ring
  Wi' echoes loud o' fame ;
My musing well, thy bonnie sel',
  And love shall be the theme.

When on Parnass', my lovely lass,
  I glance upon the fair,
I canna see a floo'r like thee,
  Thou gem beyond compare.

I canna sing, far less can bring
  My feeble tongue to tell
The loveliness, the comeliness,
  O' winsome Isabel.

Her kindly look my fancy took,
  So sweet, majestic, tender,
Did melt my soul to pay the toll
  For viewing so much grandeur.

Her ruby lips—what dainty sips
  Await the favoured lover ;
The rosy draught wi' pleasure fraught,
  A bee among the clover.

The galley slave doomed to the grave
　Would hug the tyrant's chain,
At freedom blush, nor ever wish
　To taste its sweets again.

The Floo'r o' the Dee.

Blythe warbles the lark o'er the mountain an' lea,
　The rose blushes crimson to hail the bright dawn;
But to me a' the pleasures that Nature can gi'e
　My bonnie young Jessie's the sweetest o' a'.

The dews o' the morn the pale lilies adorn,
　The violet blooms sweet wi' its modest blue e'e;
A' Nature gi'es welcome to Spring's rosy morn,
　But 't is nae sae kind as my Jessie's to me.

Thĕ oors they are lang till the day wears awa;
　But then, oh how sweet is the gloamin' to me!
At the edge o' the e'enin' love blossoms fu' braw,
　'T is then I woo Jessie, the floo'r o' the Dee.

What care I for titles or couches o' doon,
　Where the braw folk cauld poverty never dae see?
To be happy is something worth mair than a croon,
　I ask for nae mair than my Jessie can gi'e.

THE END.

www.ingramcontent.com/pod-product-compliance
Lightning Source LLC
Chambersburg PA
CBHW030847270326
41928CB00007B/1257